7 *Habits* of *H*ighly *H*ealthy People

(Antidotes for the 7 deadly sins)

by

Reverend Curry Pikkaart

Copyright © 2007 by Reverend Curry Pikkaart

7 Habits of Highly Healthy People
by Reverend Curry Pikkaart

Printed in the United States of America

ISBN 978-1-60266-695-5

All rights reserved solely by the author. The author guarantees all contents are original and do not infringe upon the legal rights of any other person or work. No part of this book may be reproduced in any form without the permission of the author. The views expressed in this book are not necessarily those of the publisher.

Unless otherwise indicated, Scripture taken from the HOLY BIBLE, NEW INTERNATIONAL VERSION®. Copyright © 1973, 1978, 1984 International Bible Society. Used by permission of Zondervan. All rights reserved.

www.xulonpress.com

CONTENTS

Introduction vii

Dedications and Acknowledgements xi

Habit #1: Do Good Works (Defeat Pride) 13

Habit #2: Practice Contentment
(Defeat Envy) 29

Habit #3: Apply the Golden Rule
(Defeat Anger) 43

Habit #4: Feed Your Hunger (Defeat Sloth) 57

Habit #5: Aim for Simplicity (Defeat Greed) 71

Habit #6: Guard Your Mind (Defeat Lust) 87

Habit: #7: Restrain Yourself (Defeat Gluttony) .. 103

Endnotes 117

INTRODUCTION

I identify so easily with Paul who wrote, "I do not understand what I do. For what I want to do I do not do, but what I hate I do...I have the desire to do what is good, but I cannot carry it out. For what I do is not the good I want to do; no, the evil I do not want to do – this I keep doing" (Romans 7:15-20). Like Paul, I am a Christian – a pastor in fact. Like Paul, I am grateful that the whole dilemma has been taken care of through Jesus Christ! Yet, like Paul, I find it so hard, and so tiring, constantly fighting the power of sin.

Does it have to be this way? If there are seven basic sins – historically called the seven deadly sins – wouldn't God provide seven basic antidotes, seven comparable virtues? This is the question that prompted me to study not only the sins, so I could understand them better, but also to search the Scriptures for the virtues. It soon became clear that the issue is one of focus. What we choose to focus on determines what we think about and ultimately what we do and how we behave. A coach, for example, tells a player going up to bat, "Now just don't strike out again!" What seed has been planted in the batter's mind? He has just increased his chances of striking out. If, on the other hand, the coach says, "Remember your good, smooth swing", what seed has been planted? He has just increased his chances of hitting the ball solidly. Similarly, if we keep concentrating on a particular sin, we increase our chances of committing the sin. If, however, we concentrate on the corresponding virtue, we increase our chances of behaving in a way that defeats the power of sin and leads to health and wholeness.

It's a known fact that once habits are developed they have staying power. The habits then become the norm for our lives. So the emphasis of this book is on developing the 7 virtuous habits that will fend off the sin and produce health. Thus the title, "7 Habits of Highly Healthy People." But rest assured, I am not ignoring the obvious – we cannot develop and maintain the habits simply by willing to do so. It begins with our will, but it depends ultimately upon Jesus Christ. And "His divine power has given us everything we need for life and godliness…you may participate in the divine nature and escape the corruption …caused by evil desires" (1 Peter 2:3-4). By carefully balancing our role of developing habits with God's super-abundant provision, you can make an exciting journey into greater spiritual health. Along the way "May (Jesus) strengthen your hearts so that you will be blameless and holy in the presence of our

God and Father when our Lord Jesus comes with all his holy ones" (1 Thessalonians 3:13)

In invite you to join the Psalmist in prayer as you begin your journey. "Search me, O God, and know my heart; test me and know my thoughts. See if there is any offensive way in me, and lead me in the way everlasting" (Psalm 139:23-24)

DEDICATION & ACKNOWLEDGEMENTS

—⋙—

This book is dedicated, with love, to my dear wife, Barb. She has sacrificed much as I have attended to my pastoral duties, and yet it has been her undying love, support, and encouragement that have sustained me and been my human rock through 33 years of ministry. And still she was willing to sacrifice more time together so I could publish this book. She has always believed in me, especially when I have not believed in myself, and without her enthusiasm and vision this book would never have become reality. Other than Jesus Christ and grace, she is truly God's richest blessing in my life.

I also express deep appreciation to Jean Otto, whose loving expertise, counsel, assistance and encouragement were invaluable in the preparation of this manuscript; to my loving mother-in-law Hazel Vugteveen, whose gracious generosity enabled me to make a firm commitment to publish this book; and to the congregations of Orchard Hill Reformed Church

(Grand Rapids) and Hope Reformed Church (South Haven), who first heard the substance of these chapters and whose honest, insightful, and enthusiastic response birthed the idea of sharing the material with a wider audience.

7 Habits of Highly Healthy People: Do Good Works
(Defeat Pride)
Genesis 11:1-9 & 1 Peter 5:5b-6

Little children find it fun, sometimes, to walk around in shoes that are too large. It helps them feel like mom or dad. It puts them into someone else's world – it helps them imagine what it would be like to be them. I know that if I put on the shoes of my second son, I'd wonder what it was like to go that much farther with each step or what it was like to kick a soccer ball with that much foot. It's fun and intriguing to ponder. But we all know that wearing shoes that are too large can eventually lead to trouble.

That's why I think that over-sized shoes are appropriate symbols for the deadly sin of pride. So often we want to walk in God's shoes, to imagine we're God. We walk around playing God until all of a sudden, because the shoes are too big, we stumble and fall. And that sounds just like pride, one of the seven deadly sins.

PRIDE IS A POWERFUL SIN

So why is pride considered a deadly sin? Pride is a powerful sin. In fact, most studies of the seven deadly sins list pride as first in rank. It's simply all encompassing. So it's important to be aware of the three basic desires at the foundation of pride.

THERE ARE THREE BASIC DESIRES AT THE FOUNDATION OF PRIDE

We find the first of these basic desires in the third chapter of Genesis. Adam and Eve have been placed in the Garden of Eden. God has told them that everything is theirs for the tending and taking – everything except for the tree of the knowledge of good and evil. So along comes Satan who tempts them: **"For God knows that when you eat of it your eyes will be opened, and you will be like God, knowing good and evil"** (Genesis 3:5). The narrative continues in verse 6: **"When the woman saw that the fruit of the tree was good for food and pleasing to the eye, and also desirable for gaining wisdom, she took some and ate it."** This is the *desire to know what God knows*. Did you ever want to see and know as God sees and knows? Have you ever asked, "Why, God?" Have you ever argued with God about His will for your life, or about one of His commandments? Have you ever desired to know more about someone else so you could lord it over them? Have you ever wished you could see inside someone's private life to know what it's really like? Have you ever grumbled about your place in life – your job, your family, your health? These are all symptoms of wanting to see, to know, and to understand like God; it's walking in God's shoes.

There's a second desire of pride: *the desire to be in charge.* Genesis 11 tells the story of building the tower of Babel. In Genesis 9 God had told Noah's family to increase in number and fill the earth. But in chapter 11 that same family decides to take charge and stay together. They do not want to spread out throughout the world: they want to be the center of the world. **"Come, let us build ourselves a city, with a tower that reaches to the heavens, so that we may make a name for ourselves and not be scattered over the face of the whole earth"** (Genesis 11:4). Have you ever tried to build your own life, to have it your own way? Ever try to promote your own name, to seek your own glory? Have you ever tried to run your own affairs, or the affairs of your children or spouse? What about trying to run your church according to your plan and your will? It's all a result of unwillingness to accept the authority and claim of God on our lives. We want to make a name for and by ourselves. It's walking in God's shoes.

The third desire of pride is the *desire to take credit* for successes in life. Think about King Nebuchadnezzar. In the 4th chapter of Daniel, we discover that the king's kingdom is very great. Daniel, in fact, tells him in verse 22: **"…your greatness has grown until it reaches the sky, and your dominion extends to distant parts of the earth."** The story continues, **"Twelve months later, as the**

king was walking on the roof of the royal palace of Babylon, he said, 'Is not this the great Babylon I have built...by my mighty power and for the glory of my majesty?'" (Daniel 4:29-30). It's a failure to recognize the sovereignty of God, who rules the nations, and to ignore that every good and perfect gift comes from Him. Did you ever think that what you have is yours, or believe that what you have is yours because you've earned it? Do you believe that you are blessed because you deserve it? Think about it – have you ever shown anybody <u>your</u> home, <u>your</u> car, <u>your</u> cottage, <u>your</u> boat, <u>your</u> family, <u>your</u> church? It's taking credit away from God. It's walking in God's shoes.

Perhaps you've answered most of the questions so far in the negative. You don't identify with such prideful thinking. But that's part of the problem of pride – we tend to think it is not an issue for us. Oswald Sanders said, "Pride is a sin of whose presence its victim is least conscious."[1] In *Mere Christianity* C. S. Lewis referred to pride as "the great sin:"

> "There is one vice of which no man in the world is free; which everyone in the world loathes when he sees it in someone else; and of which hardly any people except Christians ever imagine that they are guilty themselves...There is no fault which makes a man more unpopular, and no fault which we are more unconscious of in ourselves. And the more we have it ourselves, the more we dislike it in others...Pride leads to every

other vice...A proud man is always looking down on things and people; and, of course, as long as you're looking down, you can't see something that's above you...The first step is to realize that one is proud...If you think you are not conceited, it means you are very conceited indeed."[2]

Similarly Dante, in his "*Inferno*" shows the proud punished by carrying a huge stone that bends them over so they cannot look up.

THE MANIFESTATIONS OF PRIDE

If it is so hard to recognize pride within ourselves, how do we know for sure whether or not we are proud? We can look for the manifestations of pride. Pride shows through our lives in numerous ways. You may be *pleased with yourself.* This can take two forms. You know how good you are and rate yourself much better than so many others. But the opposite can be true as well – you can be proud of how humble you are – as evidenced by your willingness to easily admit how sinful you are.

Pride also shows up in *authority issues.* Maybe you want to be an authority over others, or want to have control not only of what you do but also of what they do and how they behave. Yet at the same time, you detest being under authority; you don't like to take orders and do things someone else's way.

Pride also surfaces in *prejudice.* Because you're so tuned in to making yourself appear good you become blind to, or cannot accept, the good in others. You find yourself shocked at, and impatient with, their faults and failures. You are very critical of others for not measuring up, yet resent any criticism that comes your way.

Rigidity is yet another manifestation of pride. You find that you are strongly opinionated – to the point of being inflexible and argumentative. No one is able to change your mind or convince you that you are wrong. You demand your way.

Then, too, even *questioning God* can be evidence of pride. Complaining about what God does or doesn't do, how He does or doesn't answer your prayers, how He does or doesn't treat you or loved ones is walking in God's shoes.

Pride might manifest itself in your life through your *hunger for recognition*, or your desire to get credit and receive affirmation. In fact, the struggle for approval is really what lies beneath our pride. We hunger for approval and praise. We worry about what others think. We believe we deserve more and better than what we have, that we are better than we're given credit for being. How, for example, do you react when another is selected for an assignment, office, or job you coveted? As C.S. Lewis said, the first step is to realize that we are, indeed, proud.

THE DESTRUCTIVENESS OF PRIDE LIES IN SEPARATION

It's important to do a thorough self-examination for pride, because of the destructiveness of pride. As

Proverbs 16:18 warns: **"Pride goes before destruction, a haughty spirit before a fall."** Why? Because *pride leads to separation from God.* What was the result of Adam and Eve partaking from the forbidden tree? It was a broken relationship with God. What was the result of building the tower of Babel? It was a broken relationship with God. We become so absorbed in tending to, building up, and focusing on our own lives, that we forget God. I could wear my son's big shoes all the time. I might even begin to manage fairly well. But at some point, I would become too comfortable and forget that they don't fit; then I might turn too quickly, or start to run, or climb steps, and I would trip, fall, and collapse. In the same vein, we can only wear God's shoes so long, and then eventually we trip, fall, and collapse. Romanian ruler Nikolai Ceausescu was one of the cruelest dictators of the 20th century. After years of viciously persecuting Christians and killing all potential threats to his power, he instructed the National Opera to produce a song in his honor. Included in this song were to be the words, "Ceausescu is good, righteous, and holy." He wanted this song sung at his 72nd birthday on January 26, 1990. Instead, he and his wife were executed a month earlier on December 25, 1989.[3] **"Pride goes before destruction, a haughty spirit before a fall."**

Pride also is destructive because it *leads to separation from others.* As someone put it, it assassinates brotherly love. Once Adam and Eve partook of the tree, they were at odds with each other. The desire of those building the tower of Babel was to keep to themselves, and not to share. It's the separation to which pride and self-centeredness lead.

As William Barclay wrote, "Pride is the ground in which all other sins grow."
Think about it. Pride grows:

- Envy – we are unable to permit the success or excellence of another
- Anger – we cannot tolerate those who frustrate our plans, purposes, and desires
- Greed – we need to possess more to be worth more and impress more;
- Lust and Gluttony – we need to satisfy ourselves (or escape from ourselves)
- Sloth – we lack love for ourselves and others

Pride is at the root of all of these sins. Pride is a powerful sin. We wear God's shoes at our own risk. **"Pride goes before destruction, a haughty spirit before a fall."**

THE ANTIDOTE FOR PRIDE IS HUMILITY

So what do we do? How can we be healthier people? The antidote for pride is humility. As Peter wrote, **"All of you, clothe yourselves with humility toward one another, because, God opposes the proud but gives grace to the humble. Humble yourselves, therefore, under God's mighty hand, that he may lift you up in due time"** (1 Peter 5:5-6).

THE MAIN CHARACTERISTICS OF HUMILITY

We are to humble ourselves. But what is the main characteristic, the main principle of humility? Humility, as commonly understood, is a delicate creature. *It is very elusive.* It's difficult to know if we have obtained it. And if we believe we have obtained it, and therefore say, "I'm a humble person," we're already starting to lean again towards pride! But the Bible gives us a different principle for humility and pride. **"This is what the LORD says: 'Let not the wise man boast of his wisdom or the strong man boast of his strength or the rich man boast of his riches, but let him who boasts boast about this: that he understands and knows me, that I am the LORD, who exercises kindness, justice and righteousness on earth, for in these I delight,' declares the LORD"** (Jeremiah 9:23-24).

We become humble when *we know Jesus Christ the Lord* - when we become like him and live obediently, exercising kindness, justice, and righteousness. It's what Paul had in mind when he wrote in Philippians 3 that he counted everything he had inherited and accomplished as garbage when compared to the greatest thing of all – knowing Jesus Christ. Paul had already painted the picture of what this knowledge means. **"Do nothing out of selfish ambition or vain conceit, but in humility consider others better than yourselves. Each of you should look not only to your own interests, but also to the interests of others. Your attitude should be the same as that** of Christ Jesus: Who, being in very nature God, did not consider equality with God something to be grasped, but made himself nothing, taking the very nature of a servant, being made in human likeness. And being found in appearance as a man, he humbled himself and became obedient to death—even death on a cross!" (Philippians 2:3-8). Through his death on the cross, Jesus fulfilled his own words that (doing nothing out of selfish ambition) He came not to be served but to serve.

THE PATH TO HUMILITY IS DOING GOOD

It's strikingly significant that when Peter summarized Jesus' life, he said, "**God anointed Jesus of Nazareth with the Holy Spirit and power, and how he went around doing good and healing all who were under the power of the devil, because God was with him**" (Acts 10:38). So the path to humility develops from doing good. The fact is that the New Testament is full of comments about and commendations for doing good.

- In writing the book of Acts Luke pointed out: "**In Joppa there was a disciple named Tabitha (which, when translated, is Dorcas), who was always doing good and helping the poor**" (Luke 9:36).
- Paul, in Romans 2:7 wrote: "**To those who by persistence in doing good seek glory, honor and immortality, he will give eternal life.**"

- In Galatians 6:9 Paul said: **"Let us not become weary in doing good, for at the proper time we will reap a harvest if we do not give up."**
- Furthermore Paul instructed Titus: **"In everything set them an example by doing what is good...Remind the people to be subject to rulers and authorities, to be obedient, to be ready to do whatever is good...And I want you to stress these things, so that those who have trusted in God may be careful to devote themselves to doing what is good. These things are excellent and profitable for everyone...Our people must learn to devote themselves to doing what is good, in order that they may provide for daily necessities and not live unproductive lives"** (Titus 2:7, 3:1, 3:8, 3:14).
- Peter wrote: **"Live such good lives among the pagans that, though they accuse you of doing wrong, they may see your good deeds and glorify God on the day he visits us...For it is God's will that by doing good you should silence the ignorant talk of foolish men"** (1 Peter 2:12, 15).

HABIT #1 – DO GOOD WORKS

I believe it's safe to say that Habit #1 is to do good works. And you and I can do good works. Peter encourages us with these words: **"His divine power has given us everything we need for life and godli-**

ness through our knowledge of him who called us by his own glory and goodness. Through these he has given us his very great and precious promises, so that through them you may participate in the divine nature and escape the corruption in the world caused by evil desires" (2 Peter 1:3-4).

WE HAVE THE POWER TO DO GOOD WORKS

We have the power to do good works. God's nature – Jesus' nature – is in our spiritual DNA. Paul, in Titus 2: 14 stated that Jesus **"...gave himself for us to redeem us from all wickedness and to purify for himself a people that are his very own, eager to do what is good."** Jesus gave himself to us and for us so we could do good works! And even now *Jesus is at work within us.* The Heidelberg Catechism affirms this when it answers question #86 by stating, "We do good because Christ by His Spirit is also renewing us to be like himself, so that in all our living we may show we are thankful to God...and so that he may be praised through us...and so that...our neighbors may be won over to Christ." Jesus, through His Holy Spirit, is working in us to help us do good works. We enter into humility as we do good works. Humility develops from doing good.

Paul, in Ephesians 2:10, made it very clear: **"For we are God's workmanship, created in Christ Jesus to do good works..."** *We are God's workmanship*: His work of art, created to do good works. We simply need to stop walking in God's shoes, and start walking in our own shoes. We are to do what we have been created to do. And what are the good works we are to do that will glorify God? The Sermon on the Mount (Matthew 5:1-12) and the life of Jesus provide much of the answer. It's not a matter of feeling, but of doing. Good works involve an attitude and action towards others and our circumstances. It amounts to loving God with all your heart and soul and mind and strength, and your neighbor as yourself. It means to live less for our own selves and more for others - to live a life of selfless service and ceaseless sacrifice. We are not showcases or trophies to be displayed and admired; we are works of art to bring glory to God. Doing good works drives us out of ourselves and towards others. That rids us of pride. Concentrate less on battling pride and more on doing good works.

GOD HAS MADE SOME GOOD WORKS COMPATIBLE WITH YOUR LIFE

God has already taken charge in helping us. God has made some good works compatible with your life. **"For we are God's workmanship, created in Christ Jesus to do good works, which God prepared in advance for us to do."** God matches the works to us and us to the works. *He prepared us in advance*. God created birds to fly – they don't run or drive cars; they fly! God has created them and the atmosphere to be compatible. So through Jesus, He has created you to do good works that He has already prepared for you to do. These words in Ephesians can be literally translated, **"God prepared them beforehand**

that we should walk in them." So walk in your own shoes! There are opportunities for good works all around you! There's a visit to a friend in the nursing home or down the street, a meal you prepare for the family in need, a listening ear you give to a troubled youth, or the encouraging word you speak to a co-worker. God even makes your circumstances opportunities for good work. Whatever your circumstance, *God has fitted you to make the contribution* that's most needed there. Cardinal John Henry Newman penned it poignantly this way:

> "God has created me to do Him some definite service; He has committed some work to me which He has not committed to another. I have my mission...Somehow I am necessary for His purposes...I am a link in a chain, a bond of connection between persons. He has not created me for naught. I shall do good, I shall do His work; I shall be an angel of peace, a preacher of truth in my own place, while not intending it, if I do but keep His commandments and serve Him in my calling... Therefore I will trust Him. Whatever, wherever I am, I can never be thrown away. If I am in sickness, my sickness may serve Him; in perplexity, my perplexity may serve Him; if I am in sorrow, my sorrow may serve Him. My sickness, or perplexity, or sorrow may be necessary causes of some great end, which is quite beyond us. He does nothing in vain; He may prolong my life, He may shorten it; He

knows what He is about. He may take away my friends, He may throw me among strangers, He may make me feel desolate, make my spirits sink, hide the future from me — still He knows what He is about."[4]

As portrayed in that great movie *Chariots of Fire*, Olympian Eric Liddell said, "I believe God made me for a purpose...and when I run, I feel His pleasure." When you walk in your own shoes, and do the good works God has already prepared for you to do, you will enter into humility and *feel God's pleasure*. Simply begin each day by praying, "Father, thank you for the good works already prepared for me this day. Thank you that they are just waiting for me to step into and experience. Help me to recognize them and then to walk boldly in my shoes, for your glory. Amen."

The day before I finished editing this chapter, a nearby Christian Radio Station had just completed a "Pay Back" day. During that day the station encouraged listeners to go to a drive-in (or regular) restaurant, and to pay for the person behind them. The day I edited this chapter, therefore, was 'report day', when listeners and others called in their experiences. The accounts were grace-filled, amazing, moving, and several times brought me to the brink of tears. Even as I was typing the words, "...do the good works God has already prepared for you to do, you will enter into humility and feel God's pleasure," I was hearing its truth expressed in the lives of the callers. It was, for me, the Lord's, powerful and personal affirmation of the power of good works. Thank you, Lord.[5]

7 Habits of Highly Healthy People: Practice Contentment
(Defeat Envy)
1 Samuel 18:1-15 & Philippians 4:10-13

—⁂—

There is a fable in which Satan's agents were failing in their various attempts to draw into sin a holy man who lived as a hermit in the desert of Northern Africa. Every attempt had met with failure; so Satan, angered with the incompetence of his subordinates, became personally involved in the case. He said, "The reason you have failed is that your methods are too crude for one such as this. Watch this." He then approached the holy man with great care and whispered softly in his ear, "Your brother has just been made Bishop of Alexandria." Instantly the holy man's face showed that Satan had been successful: a great scowl formed over his mouth and his eyes tightened up. "Envy," said Satan, "is often our best weapon against those who seek holiness." Good fable, with a good moral. But is it true?

THE NEED FOR A HABIT

We can find out by further examining the need for a habit. One of the best places to look in the Bible for a picture of envy is 1 Samuel 18, the story of Saul.

THERE IS A PICTURE OF ENVY

It was a day of great rejoicing. Israel, largely due to lack of courage, had been on the brink of defeat. Then young David slew the giant Goliath and the enemy Philistine troops had tried to run away in fear. But the newly energized Israelite troops pursued, overtook, and defeated them. Their march home was, therefore, not one of humiliation and defeat but of rejoicing and triumph. Throngs of people, especially women, lined the roads as the army marched home. The people were grateful for the unexpected victory and for David and the armies of Saul. It was truly a day of rejoicing for everyone.

Everyone, that is, except for Saul. He heard the crowds honoring David and he couldn't handle it. He was the king and he believed he should get the credit. He wanted the adulation and popularity that was being given to David. It was the turning point in Saul's life. His envy of David turned to bitterness, anger, and perhaps even hatred. Soon thereafter Saul tried to kill the young hero David. Saul's life and kingship were on the way downhill. Envy is the best weapon against those who seek holiness.

This passage, therefore, becomes for us a lesson on envy. And just what is envy? How do we define it? *Envy is a desire to possess what another has, or at the least to make sure they lose it.* "If I can't have it, then neither can you!" Notice that envy is slightly different than jealousy. Jealousy is guarding what one already has for fear of losing it. For example, let's say that Peter and Pauline have been dating. Pauline suddenly goes out with Herman. Peter is not envious – he is jealous. He fears losing her. If, on the other hand, Peter has been eying Pauline, but they have not been dating when she goes out with Herman, then Peter is envious. He wants what Herman has, or wants them to have a horrible time so Pauline will look at him.

Scripture is filled with many accounts of envy. Cain killed Abel because he desired the approval God gave to Abel. Joseph's brothers sold Joseph into slavery because they wanted the special attention and favor their father poured out on Joseph. Daniel's associates were envious of the relationship Daniel had with the King, so they set up a law and trapped Daniel. As a result Daniel was thrown into a den of lions. Pilate knew Jesus had done no wrong, but out of envy he delivered Jesus up to be crucified. *Envy is a desire to possess what another has, or at the least to make sure they lose it.* "If I can't have it, then neither can you!"

THERE ARE DEVASTATING EFFECTS OF ENVY

Are you beginning to see the devastating effects of envy? First, *it removes joy* from one's life because envy is the opposite of gratitude and gratitude is the seedbed of joy. Envy does not allow us to be grateful for what we have or for who we are. According to Thomas Watson, "Discontent keeps a man from enjoying what he doth possess. A drop or two of vinegar will sour a whole glass of wine."[1] Secondly, *envy consumes us*; it eats us up and destroys us. We talk about someone who is "green with envy." That's appropriate, because, in fact, extreme envy does affect the envier physically. It destroys his emotion and even restricts blood flow. The wise preacher was right: **"A heart at peace gives life to the body, but envy rots the bones"** (Proverbs 14:30). Third, *envy blinds us*. It keeps us from appreciating the good and beautiful in others, as well as in ourselves. And that keeps us from seeing the goodness and greatness of the very God who apportioned His gifts among us. As the Rev. Billy Graham has poignantly written: "Envy can ruin reputations, split churches, and cause murders. Envy can shrink our circle of friends, ruin our business, and dwarf our souls...I have seen hundreds cursed by it."[2]

THERE ARE SIGNS OF ENVY

So beware of the signs of envy. How can you know if envy has crept into your heart? Have you ever had an *attitude of sour grapes* at the accomplishments or gifts of another? Have you ever *put someone else down* or overly criticized them when positive attention came their way? Do you ever *compare yourself with others* only to feel poorly about yourself? When you see persons more successful or popular than you, do you wish to be more like them, or do you wish they would fall from grace? Have you found yourself *rejoicing with those who weep and weeping with those who rejoice*? Welcome to the world of envy.

THERE IS A SOURCE FOR ENVY

But why is envy so prevalent? Why does it strike us all? What is the source of envy? Jesus made it very clear: all sin *originates in the heart*: **"What comes out of a man is what makes him 'unclean.' For from within, out of men's hearts, come evil thoughts, sexual immorality, theft, murder, adultery, greed, malice, deceit, lewdness, envy, slander, arrogance and folly. All these evils come from inside and make a man 'unclean'** (Mark 7:20-23). We need a change of heart. Paul put it this way **"...just as Christ was raised from the dead through the glory of God the Father, we too may live a new life"** (Rom. 6:4). So the issue becomes *a change in heart*.

THE DEVELOPMENT OF THE HABIT

To change our hearts, we can consider the development of the habit. As Peter wrote: **"Therefore, rid yourselves of all malice and all deceit, hypocrisy, envy, and slander of every kind...His divine power has given us everything we need for life and godliness..."** (1 Peter 2:1 & 2 Peter 1:3). We see this at work in the story of Paul. As he wrote to the Philippians he was a prisoner in Rome, chained to guards 24/7. He was under a possible death sentence. Yet from this environment Paul wrote, **"Rejoice in the lord always. I will say it again: Rejoice! ... I have learned to be content whatever the circumstances..." (Philippians 4:4 & 11).**

HABIT #2 - PRACTICE CONTENTMENT

What a contrast to Saul. Saul had everything, but his heart was filled with envy. Paul had nothing and he rejoiced. What's the difference? It's a difference in the heart. Paul's words to the Philippians teach us that, as opposed to envy, *contentment is a sense of well-being, the assurance that everything will be all right*.

PAUL TEACHES ABOUT CONTENTMENT

Paul then continues by offering some teachings on contentment. First, *contentment is learned*. We are not born with it, we cannot buy it; it is learned. Twice Paul stresses this: **"...I have learned to be content whatever the circumstances... I have learned the secret of being content in any and every situation..." (Philippians 4:11-12).** The word for "learned" is literally "been initiated into." The experiences of life are our initiation into contentment. No matter what your situation right now, ask yourself, "How is this initiating me into contentment? What can I learn about contentment?"

Realize that this imprisonment was not Paul's only hardship or struggle. Paul had gradually learned this contentment. As he told the Corinthian church:

> "Are they servants of Christ? (I am out of my mind to talk like this.) I am more. I have worked much harder, been in prison more frequently, been flogged more severely, and been exposed to death again and again. Five times I received from the Jews the forty lashes minus one. Three times I was beaten with rods, once I was stoned, three times I was shipwrecked, I spent a night and a day in the open sea, I have been constantly on the move. I have been in danger from rivers, in danger from bandits, in danger from my own countrymen, in danger from Gentiles; in danger in the city, in danger in the country, in danger at sea; and in danger from false brothers. I have labored and toiled and have often gone without sleep; I have known hunger and thirst and have often gone without food; I have been cold and naked. Besides everything else, I face daily the pressure of my concern for all the churches" (2 Corinthians 11:23-28). Later he wrote more: "To keep me from becoming conceited because of these surpassingly great revelations, there was given me a thorn in my flesh, a messenger of Satan, to torment me. Three times I pleaded with the Lord to take it away from

me. But he said to me, "My grace is sufficient for you, for my power is made perfect in weakness." Therefore I will boast all the more gladly about my weaknesses, so that Christ's power may rest on me. That is why, for Christ's sake, I delight in weaknesses, in insults, in hardships, in persecutions, in difficulties. For when I am weak, then I am strong" (2 Corinthians 12:7-10).

Likewise, through what happens to us and around us *we can be initiated into the secret of God's power and presence*. Every circumstance, every situation, is a lesson. It is a lesson from God about what's most important in life.

The second thing Paul teaches about contentment is that *contentment is attitudinal, not circumstantial.* Contentment does not rely on our circumstances, but on our attitude. **"I am not saying this because I am in need, for I have learned to be content whatever the circumstances. I know what it is to be in need, and I know what it is to have plenty. I have learned the secret of being content in any and every situation, whether well fed or hungry, whether living in plenty or in want"** (Philippians 4:11-12). Contentment - a sense of well-being, the assurance that everything will be all right – comes from knowing what is important in life. And things (the stuff that we envy) are, ultimately, not all that important. The comedy film *Cool Runnings* is about the first-ever Jamaican bobsled team to go to the Olympics. John

Candy starred as their coach, a former gold medallist who had become a hero to the Jamaican team. Later in the story the coach's dark past surfaced. Following his gold medal performance, he competed again in another Olympics, but broke the rules by weighting the U.S. sled, thus bringing disgrace on himself and this team. One of the Jamaican bobsledders could not understand why anyone who had already won a gold medal would cheat. Finally he asked the coach why. The coach replied, "I had to win. I learned something. If you are not happy without a gold medal, you won't be happy with it." Contentment - a sense of well-being, the assurance that everything will be all right – comes from knowing what is important in life. And things (the stuff that we envy) are, ultimately, not all that important.

In that same spirit Paul wrote to Timothy: **"But godliness with contentment is great gain. For we brought nothing into the world, and we can take nothing out of it. But if we have food and clothing, we will be content with that"** (1 Tim. 6:6-8). As Rick Warren once pointed out, our kids aren't born with Nike or Reeboks on their feet. So those are just plusses, extras, and bonuses along the road of life. Quite frankly, I have never yet seen a hearse pulling a U-Haul trailer. We begin and end with nothing. You see – *our perspective controls our attitude*. We can be either thermometers that reflect the temperature around us, or we can be thermostats that set the temperature. Such is the belief of a poet:

> "I've never made a fortune;
> And I'll never make one now,
> But it really doesn't matter;
> Cause I'm happy anyhow.
> As I go along my journey;
> I'm reaping better than I sow.
> I'm drinking from the saucer;
> Cause my cup has overflowed.
> I don't have a lot of riches;
> And sometimes the going's tough,
> But when I've got my kids to love me;
> I think I'm rich enough.
> I'll just thank God for the blessings;
> That his mercy has bestowed,
> I'm drinking from the saucer;
> Cause my cup has overflowed.
> If you give me strength and courage;
> When the way grows steep and rough
> I'll not ask for other blessings;
> I'm already blessed enough.
> May I never be too busy;
> To help another with his load,
> Then I'll be drinking from the saucer;
> Cause my cup has overflowed."[3]

Be a thermostat. Burning these verses into your heart will help you: **"And we know that in all things God works for the good of those who love him..."** (Romans 8:28) and **"...be content with what you have, because God has said, 'Never will I leave you; never will I forsake you'"** (Hebrews 13:5). *It's not what we have but who has us that matters most.*

In his book *Reaching for the Invisible God* Philip Yancey points out a key verse that helped me grasp this thought. He quotes Jesus: **"Are not two sparrows sold for a penny? ... Yet not one of them will fall to the ground apart from the will of your Father."** He then mentions that the Greek text omits the reference to the will. It reads: **"Yet not one of them will fall to the ground apart from your Father."** Catch the difference? As Jacques Ellul pointed out: "In the one case, God wills the death of the sparrow, in the other death does not take place without God being present. In other words, death comes according to natural laws, but God lets nothing in is creation die without being there, without being the comfort and strength and hope and support of that which dies. At issue is the presence of God, not the will of God."[4]

Contentment - a sense of well-being, the assurance that everything will be all right – comes from knowing what is important in life. And what's important is our perspective about God's power and presence.

The third thing that Paul teaches about contentment is that *contentment is relational*. So it's not surprising that Paul next states: **"I can do everything through him who gives me strength"** (vs. 13). Contentment comes from a personal relationship with Jesus Christ. There is no need to worry about what we do not have when we know what (or who) we do have! Contentment is not some form of self-sufficiency. No – the Bible tells us that our *sufficiency comes from a relationship with the always-present*

Jesus Christ. Dr. Tim Brown, Professor of Preaching at Western Theological Seminary, taught at Hope College prior to his seminary position. He told the story of one of his students, named Tim VanderVeen. Tim graduated from Hope in the early 90's. Some years later he was diagnosed with leukemia. For three years it was his battle. Finally he went to the hospital to die. Dr. Brown shared his experience:

> "I walked into the room. His mother was sitting in the corner crying. You can't blame her. Tim was lying on his side. They had positioned the pillows between his skinny little legs. His hair wasn't curly anymore. There wasn't enough energy for him to look at me, so I got down on one knee so I could look him eyeball to eyeball. I said, 'Hi Tim.' He said, 'Hi, Tim.' There was this long, awkward pause. I'd been a pastor for 20 years, and I still didn't know what to say. He broke the silence. He said, 'I've learned something.' … I said, 'Tell me, partner, what you have learned.' He said, 'I have learned that life is not like a VCR.' Now I didn't get it then anymore than you're getting it now. So I said, 'I don't get it. What do you mean?' He said, 'It's not like a VCR; you can't fast forward the bad parts…But I have learned that Jesus Christ is in every frame, and right now that's just enough.'"[5]

Contentment - a sense of well-being, the assurance that everything will be all right – comes from knowing what is important in life. And what's important is our perspective about God's power and presence. JESUS CHRIST IS IN EVERY FRAME OF OUR LIVES. Nothing else matters. It's all – He's all – we need. Believing that, we can practice contentment and say good-bye to envy. Just remember, no matter the current frame of your life, no matter what's happening to or around you, Jesus Christ is with you. He's on your side. He'll work for your good. And He'll never leave you. Never. Ever. You can do everything through Him who gives you strength.

May this beloved hymn bolster your faith and encourage your heart of contentment.

Day by Day

"Day by day and with each passing moment,
Strength I find to meet my trials here;
Trusting in my Father's wise bestowment,
I've no cause for worry or for fear.
He whose heart is kind beyond all measure
Gives unto each day what He deems best –
Lovingly, it's part of pain and pleasure,
Mingling toil with peace and rest.

Every day the Lord Himself is near me
With a special mercy for each hour;
All my cares He fain would bear, and cheer me,
He whose name is Counselor and Power.
The protection of His child and treasure
Is a charge that on Himself He laid;
"As your days, your strength shall be in measure",
This the pledge to me He made.

Help me then in every tribulation
So to trust Your promises, O Lord,
That I lose not faith's consolation
Offered me within Your holy Word.
Help me, Lord, when toil and trouble meeting,
E'er to take, as from a father's hand,
One by one, the days, the moments fleeting,
Till I reach the promised land." [6]

7 Habits of Highly Healthy People: Apply the Golden Rule
(Defeat Anger)
Matthew 18:21-35

One cold winter evening a man suffered a heart attack. After being admitted to the hospital he asked the nurse to call his daughter, who was the only family he had. When the nurse talked to the daughter, the daughter became very upset and said, "You must not let him die! You see, Dad and I had a terrible argument almost a year ago. I haven't seen him since. All these months I've wanted to go to him for forgiveness. The last thing I said to him was, 'I hate you.' The daughter began to cry, and then said, "I'm coming now. I'll be there in thirty minutes." Shortly thereafter her father went into cardiac arrest. As they worked to revive him the nurse prayed, "Oh God, his daughter is coming. Don't let it end this way." But the father died. Soon the nurse noticed a doctor talking to the daughter outside the room, and she could see the hurt in her face. The nurse took the daughter aside and said, "I'm sorry." The daughter responded, "I never hated him, you know. I loved him, and now I want to go see him." So the nurse escorted her into the room, where the daughter immediately buried her face in the sheets as she said good-bye to her father. The nurse noticed a scrap of paper on the bed table. She picked it up and read it. It said, "My dearest Janie, I forgive you. I pray you will also forgive me. I know that you love me. I love you, too. Daddy."

What a poignant picture of the devastation and pain that anger causes! As author Frederick Buechner wrote, "Of the Seven Deadly Sins, anger is possibly the most fun. To lick your wounds, to smack your lips over grievances long past, to roll over your tongue the prospect of bitter confrontations still to come, to savor to the last toothsome morsel both the pain you are given and the pain you are giving back – in many ways it is a feast fit for a king. The chief drawback is that what you are wolfing down is yourself. The skeleton at the feast is you."[1] There is no doubt we need to develop a habit to control and overcome our anger. And while people get angry for many reasons and at many things, most often anger is aimed, directly or indirectly, at some other person.

THE ISSUE OF MERCY

Dealing with anger puts the focus on the issue of mercy. Looking at Matthew 18 we discover that Jesus had just taught how to reconcile relationships (15-18), and what to do if all attempts at reconciliation failed. In Peter's mind, that prompted a legitimate question about forgiveness.

A LEGITIMATE QUESTION ABOUT FORGIVENESS

In verse 21 we read: **"Then Peter came to Jesus and asked, 'Lord, how many times shall I forgive my brother when he sins against me? Up to seven times?'"** Peter's question was, while a little foreign to us, *based on Jewish law*. Peter knew without question that he must forgive. But Judaism taught that three times was enough to show a forgiving spirit – the Rabbis believed that repeat offenders may not really be repenting at all. So Peter was simply responding out of his background and tradition. So his offer of seven times (seven being the number of perfection) was above and beyond what was required.

Peter's question was also a *logical question*. In fact, you and I have probably asked it more than once.

"How many times must I forgive him?

"I've forgiven her so many times, and it doesn't seem to make any difference? "Doesn't there come a point when he doesn't deserve forgiveness?"

We've all been hurt by other people – sometimes repeatedly. No one gets through life without such injury. So Peter's question, which is our question, is legitimate. How many times must we forgive someone?

A SURPRISING PARABLE

In response to Peter's question, Jesus told a surprising parable. He introduced the story by answering Peter's question about how many times we are to forgive someone: **"I tell you, not seven times, but seventy-seven times"** (vs. 22). In other words, forgive an unlimited number of times. Forgiveness has no limits. Then Jesus proceeded to tell what life in His kingdom is like. The king wanted to settle accounts with his servants, as any good businessperson would do. The servant owed him an amount that he could never, ever be able to pay. But when the servant pleaded for mercy – and even made a promise he could never keep – the king forgave the debt. What a break for the servant! What a chance for new life! As he went forth rejoicing he came across one of his own servants, who owed him a mere pittance. He forcefully demanded payment, only to hear the same plea he had just given to the king. But rather than forgive he threw the man into prison, where he had no hope of earning the money to repay the debt. When the king received word of these actions he called the servant back into his presence. **"Then the master called the servant in. 'You wicked servant,' he said, 'I canceled all that debt of yours because you begged me to. Shouldn't you have had mercy on your fellow servant just as I had on you?' In anger his master turned him over to the jailers to be tortured, until he should pay back all he owed."** That's where the story ends. Then, to be sure the disciples got the message Jesus concluded:

"This is how my heavenly Father will treat each of you unless you forgive your brother from your heart."

Jesus wanted to be sure two lessons were learned.

First, *anger towards another is a rejection of God's mercy.* To receive mercy but not offer mercy invalidates any original mercy received. That's one of the problems of anger towards others – it is rebellion against the very mercy Jesus died to offer.

Second, *the forgiven must seek to forgive.* It's not that we earn forgiveness by forgiving others. God doesn't relate to us in a tit-for-tat fashion. Rather, Jesus is teaching that since anger is rejection of His mercy, God will respond by withdrawing His mercy. In other words, we block His mercy when we refuse to forgive. We are to make every effort to offer the mercy of Christ to those who hurt and offend us and to fervently pray for the strength and wisdom to avoid revenge and overcome hate.

SOME DEEPER QUESTIONS

But I don't think that's the end of the discussion. I believe the whole scene raises some deeper questions. Jesus is calling us to account. He wants us to know how we stand in relationship to Him. He wants us to know what we owe Him. And we owe Him an infinite debt that we can never pay.

HOW DO YOU WANT GOD TO TREAT YOU?

So question number one is, how do you want God to treat you? Do you want Him to give you only what you deserve? Or do you want Him to cut you a little slack while you figure out a way to repay your unpayable debt? Or do you want Him to heal you, help you, and forgive you? Are there some promises you're willing to make to move Him towards mercy?

HOW HAS GOD TREATED YOU?

Question number two, then, is how has God treated you? The key is to stop focusing on what someone else has done to you and instead focus on what God has done for you. But that's hard because we want revenge – or in the least, judgment or punishment on the one who hurt us. He or she needs to face the music and pay the price. They are not worthy of forgiveness. And it's true – they probably aren't. But then, are you? And hasn't somebody already paid the price? **"The wages of sin is death, but the gift of God is eternal life through Jesus Christ our Lord"** (Rom. 6:23). Remember the old hymn?

> "Nothing in my hand I bring,
> Simply to thy cross I cling;
> Naked, come to Thee for dress,
> Helpless, look to Thee for grace;
> Foul, I to the fountain fly,
> Wash me, Savior, or I die!"[2]

HOW WILL YOU TREAT OTHERS?

This brings us to question number three. Knowing how God has treated you, how will you treat others? As Max Lucado has written, "You will never be called upon to give anyone more grace than God has already given you."[3] Think about it; how much grace has He given you? ... Now offer that to others. It's not easy. C. S. Lewis wrote, "Everyone says forgiveness is a lovely idea, until they have something to forgive."[4] No, it's not easy. But the Bible tells us how to do so.

HABIT #3 – APPLY JESUS' GOLDEN RULE

First, adopt and practice *the golden rule* found in Matthew 7:12: **"Do unto others as you would have them do unto you."** Are you angry because of what someone did to you? How would you like for them to have treated you? Treat them that way. I do not mean to imply a wishy-washy "Don't worry – everything's OK" type of attitude. There are many times when an offender needs to face up to the consequences of his actions. What we're dealing with is our personal attitude towards others. We are not responsible for the event or person that provokes our anger, but we are responsible for how we respond once anger starts welling up within us. How do you want to be treated? Treat others that way.

In her autobiographical book *Climbing*, missionary Rosalind Goforth tells of the internal rage she harbored against someone who had greatly harmed her and her husband, Jonathan. It was a serious injury that the couple would never afterward talk about, but while Jonathan seemed to easily forgive the offender, Rosalind refused to do so. For more than a year, she would not talk to nor recognize that person who lived near them on their missionary station in China. Four years passed and the matter remained unsolved and, to an extent, forgotten. One day the Goforths were traveling by train to a religious meeting elsewhere in China. For months, Rosalind had felt a lack of power in her Christian life and ministry, and in her train compartment she bowed her head and cried to God to be filled with the Holy Spirit. "Unmistakably clear came the Inner Voice, 'Write to (the one toward whom I felt hatred and unforgiveness) and ask forgiveness for the way you have treated him.' My whole soul cried out 'Never!' Again I prayed as before, and again the Inner Voice spoke clearly as before. Again I cried out in my heart, 'Never; never. I will never forgive him!' When for the third time this was repeated, I jumped to my feet and said to myself, 'I'll give it all up, for I'll never, never forgive!' One day afterward, Rosalind was reading to the children from "Pilgrim's Progress". It was the passage in which a man in a cage moans, "I have grieved the Spirit. And He is gone: I have provoked God to anger, and He has left me." Instantly a terrible conviction came upon her, and for two days and nights she felt in terrible despair. Finally, talking late at night with a fellow missionary, a young widower, she burst into sobs and told him the whole story. "But Mrs. Goforth," he said, "Are you willing to write the letter?" At length she replied, "Yes." "Then go at once and write it." Rosalind jumped up, ran into the house, and wrote a few lines of humble apology for her actions, without any reference to his. The joy and peace of her Christian life returned. "From that time," Rosalind wrote in her autobiography, "I have never dared not to forgive." [5]

It sounds very much like the attitude that Jesus introduced, which we now call the golden rule.

Second, Christians, of all people, can apply the golden rule because we can *adopt incompatible behavior*. Incompatible means that there are some things that cannot exist together. Oil and water don't mix. Water and flame don't mix. And anger and forgiveness don't mix. *If we exercise forgiveness, there is no room for anger.* That's why Paul wrote **"Be kind and compassionate to one another, forgiving each other, just as in Christ God forgave you"** (Ephesians 4:32). Forgiveness is surrendering my right to hurt you back if you hurt me. It means not returning tit-for-tat. So you've been lied to, gossiped about, betrayed, maligned, or abused? Adopt incompatible behavior. You can because you are able to "...

be strong in the grace we have in Christ Jesus...Be kind and compassionate to one another, forgiving each other, just as in Christ God forgave you" (Ephesians 4:32). God never asks us to do anything that He has not equipped us to do – even when it comes to forgiving others.

The third step in treating others in a healthy manner is to *assess your relationships*. It begins by seriously analyzing where you really stand in your relationship *with Jesus Christ*. The problem with the servant in Jesus' parable was that he still felt unforgiven; he hadn't really let the mercy of the king settle in his heart. Hebrews 12:15 states: **"See to it that no one misses the grace of God and that no bitter root grows up to cause trouble and defile many."** Similarly, Max Lucado has written, "Where the grace of God is missed, bitterness is born. But where the grace of God is embraced, forgiveness flourishes." He then points to 2 Timothy 2:1: **"...be strong in the grace we have in Christ Jesus."** Paul doesn't tell Timothy to be strong in Bible study or prayer or giving – but in grace. Then Lucado states, "The longer we walk in the garden, the more likely we are to smell like flowers. The more we immerse ourselves in grace, the more likely we are to give grace."[6] By focusing on Jesus Christ and the cross, you can adopt behavior that is incompatible with anger. Quit concentrating on what someone else has done to you and concentrate on what Jesus has done for you.

The next relationship to assess is your relationship *with others*. At whom are you angry? With whom do you have a broken relationship? Whom do you need to forgive? What will you do?

YOU HAVE A CHOICE

Always remember – you have a choice. You can respond in anger. But understand that your anger is as damaging to you as it is to the offender who hurt you. If you fail to forgive, your anger builds. Soon you begin to think and do negative things toward him. Eventually the hurt turns to hate and you soon hate anyone like him. So people say things like:

"All men are jerks.
"You can't ever trust a woman.
"Every preacher is lazy and dishonest.
"All Christians are prejudiced."

The hurt has become rage because, by failing to exercise forgiveness, you have let it fester.

You can choose anger or you can choose forgiveness. It's true that your mercy may never change others; but it will change you. Michael Wilkins, in his commentary on this parable, wrote:

> "I've mentioned elsewhere that I was raised by a stepfather who caused my family and me a great deal of pain. He left our family when I was in my early teens, and I carried a deep animosity toward him for years. When I was in Vietnam, my animosity became almost obsessive, and I vowed that the first time I

saw him on my return, I would kill him. I would make him pay for what he had done to our family. I returned a few months later and within a year had become a Christian. My world began to change, and I put that stepfather out of my mind. I had not thought about him much until about four years later, when he suddenly showed up where my wife and I and our little girl were living. He had tracked us down. My wife, being the loving person she is, invited him in. As we sat and talked politely, that vow came to my mind. I then told him, 'I made a vow in Vietnam that the first time I saw you, I would kill you. Today is that day' I will never forget the look of terror that came over his face. He started to sweat and slide down on the couch. I went on, 'But I now know that I'm no better a person than you. God has forgiven me. And if he can forgive a sinner like me, I can forgive you. I will not allow you to hurt my family again, so don't think that this is made out of weakness. Rather, I forgive you because I have been forgiven.'"[7]

So the choice is always yours - anger or forgiveness. I challenge and remind you: "The longer (you) walk in the garden, the more likely (you) are to smell like flowers. The more (you) immerse (yourself in grace), the more likely (you) are to give grace." I invite you to turn to Jesus.

Pray the words of this hymn as you turn to Jesus:

> "Come, O Fount of every blessing,
> Tune my heart to sing Your grace;
> Streams of mercy, never ceasing,
> Call for songs of loudest praise.
> Teach me some melodious sonnet
> Sung by flaming tongues above;
> Praise the mount – I'm fixed upon it –
> Mount of Your redeeming love.
>
> Here I raise to You an altar –
> Hither by Your help I'm come;
> And I hope by Your good pleasure
> Safely to arrive at home.
> Jesus sought me when a stranger
> Wandering from the fold of God;
> He to rescue me from danger
> Interposed His precious blood.
>
> O to grace how great a debtor
> Daily I'm constrained to be!
> Let Your goodness like a fetter
> Bind my wandering heart to Thee.

> Prone to wander – Lord, I feel it –
> Prone to leave the God I love;
> Here's my heart – O take and seal it,
> Seal it for Your courts above.[8]

7 Habits Of Highly Healthy People: Feed Your Hunger
(Defeat Sloth)
Proverbs 24:30-34 & Luke 7:36-50

—⁕—

A *Peanuts* comic strip shows Charlie Brown and Schroeder walking and having a deep discussion. Schroeder asks, "Is Snoopy a hunting dog?" Says Charlie, "I guess he is in a way." Schroeder continues, "What does he hunt, animals or birds?" Neither," replies Charlie. "What he hunts for mostly is an easier way of life." Sound familiar? I wonder if you have ever hunted or wished for an easier way of life? How about for an easier faith or religious life? I wonder if you might just be affected by sloth.

THERE IS A PICTURE OF SLOTH

To assist in discovering whether or not you are affected by sloth, it's helpful to look at a picture of sloth. Of the seven deadly sins, this is the one with which we're probably most unfamiliar. We're not sure we'd recognize it, except in it's most common form of laziness.

TEST YOUR RECOGNITION OF SLOTH

So we need to test our recognition of sloth. Here's a little self-test.

Have you ever felt:
- Worthless?
- Hopeless about life?
- Too tired to do much of anything?
- You weren't doing what you ought to have been doing?

Have you ever been at the point:
- Where, to have a good time, you'd rather sit around than do something active?
- Where you wanted to quit and had to force yourself to keep going?
- Where you were angry with yourself, or low-spirited and sad most of the time?

Have you ever found:
- Your spiritual disciplines difficult?
- Your times of worship, prayer, and Bible reading were too hard?
- Your will weak – and you didn't seem to care – or even notice?
- You were dissatisfied or angry with God for not giving to you the feelings of peace and happiness?

If you answered, "Yes", to any of these questions, you may well have been, or be slothful. (Please see endnote [1])

UNDERSTAND THE PROPERTIES OF SLOTH

To probe further we need to understand the properties of sloth. The word 'sloth' comes from two words that mean negligence, apathy, and aimless indifference to one's responsibilities to God and others, which leads to sadness and despair. It usually involves avoiding what needs to be done or doing it listlessly – just going through the motions. As the *Pocket Catholic* Catechism defines it, "The slothful person is unwilling to do what God wants because of the effort it takes to do it. Sloth becomes a sin when it slows down and even brings to a halt the energy we must expend in using the means to salvation."[2] In essence, it's *the absence of passion.* This means sloth is not limited to someone being lazy about work or keeping up his house and yard. It is just as often a spiritual malady. Consider, for example, the Pharisee in Luke 7:36-50. At first glance, it appears that he was doing the noble, faithful thing; he was, after all, hosting Jesus. But upon further review it's obvious his love for and dedication to Jesus was not his main agenda. His passion was to check out, and perhaps trap, Jesus. It was the woman, a prostitute, who showered Jesus with true affection, love, and devotion. She was passionate about Jesus. She understood who she was and who Jesus was; the Pharisee was numb to who Jesus was.

Have you ever had Novacaine at the dentist's office? It numbs part of your mouth. It desensitizes that area. Similarly, sloth is *a form of numbness.* It is a lack of sensitivity to Jesus that numbs us to the fullest possible experience of God.

THERE ARE THREE CAUSES OF SLOTH

I realize that few, if any of us, set out to be slothful. We just don't say, "Today I think I'll be numb to God" or "I think I'll be slothful today since I really don't want to experience God." So what happens to us? How does sloth develop? There are, at least, three causes of sloth.

THE PAIN OF LIFE

First, there is the pain of life. It is sometimes very difficult to deal with the pain in our lives. None of us have been or will be pain free. Some have much more pain than others. There are broken relationships, job pressures and job loss, strained family relationships, physical infirmities, lack of popularity, financial difficulties, unanswered prayer, struggles for sexual fulfillment and identity, loneliness or lack of friends, the aging process, unending guilt – the list could go on and on. To complicate matters, we often do not want to admit we are in pain. We may not even share it with God because we're too proud or too ashamed to do so. A vast majority of drug or alcohol addicts eventually admit that they turned to their drug of choice because it numbed them from their particular pain. Numbness is certainly preferable to pain – that's why we use Novacaine and anesthesia! We like to reduce the pain. That's why when I had my heart surgery I welcomed the anesthesia – numbness was preferable to pain! But in our life of faith, when we try to hide our pain by failing to be honest about or deal with it, we become numb to Jesus and we lose our passion. As the Apostle John put it in Revelation 2:4: **"You have forsaken your first love."**

THE PACE OF LIFE

A second cause of sloth is the pace of life. We are not inactive people. In fact, most of us are busier than ever. Yet isn't it ironic that in this age of technology, when we have more time saving devices than ever before in history, we are busier than ever before in history? Rather than use the time saved by our devices to relax and rest we use it to do more and get more. Why is it this way? It's another way of hiding pain, of ignoring the issues of life. If we stay busy we don't have time to think or feel. It's also a subtle way of hiding from and dealing with God. As Peter Kreeft wrote, "We are hiding ourselves; we are hiding the God-sized hole in our hearts, the hole in the foundation of our existence...There is a deep spiritual sorrow at the heart of modern civilization because it is the first civilization in all of history that does not know who it is or why it is, that cannot answer the three great questions: Where did I come from? Why am I here? and Where am I going?"[3] We have little time to enjoy life and even less time to enjoy God. We think that, if we stay busy, we won't need to deal with God or His judgment on the pace of our lives. But we have not listened to the words of St. Augustine: "He who has God has everything; he who has everything but God has nothing; and he who has God plus everything does not have any more than he who has God alone."[4]

APATHY TOWARDS LIFE

The third cause of sloth is the apathy towards life. Because we are so numb and so busy we have no desire, time, or energy to invest in the real issues of life. We do not, therefore, spend time investing in our marital relationships, so the feeling of love dies; that's one reason for the large number of divorces and increased amount of abuse. We fail to discipline children because it takes time and energy we do not have; so children grow up undisciplined and with no boundaries. We live in cloistered neighborhoods because getting to know our neighbors requires the very time and energy we do not have. We fail to pursue any purpose in life because to do so requires reflection and time; that partially explains why books like Rick Warren's *40 Days of Purpose* are such big sellers. We can handle 40 days, but more than that, well…we're not so sure. So we carry our pace of life over into our spiritual life as well. We just simply have very little time to pursue a relationship with Jesus Christ. We try to break down our devotions into bite-sized chunks and our prayers into intermittent arrows; in fact we are uncomfortable if we spend too long alone with Christ, or even in worship. After all, there are places to go, people to see, and things to do. And then we wonder why we have so little inner peace and why it's so hard to be content. To put it succinctly, we fail to grasp our hunger for God; we fail to recognize that our hearts are restless until they find their rest in God.

Sadly, we have forgotten the words of Jesus: **"I know your deeds, that you are neither cold nor hot. I wish you were either one or the other! So, because you are lukewarm—neither hot nor cold—I am about to spit you out of my mouth. You say, 'I am rich; I have acquired wealth and do not need a thing.' But you do not realize that you are wretched, pitiful, poor, blind and naked"** (Revelation 3:15-18). Heironymus Bosch painted pictures of the seven deadly sins. William Willimon points out that in the picture of sloth he has a man sitting comfortably in a cushioned chair before a warm fire, his dog curled up at his feet, the very image of Dutch bourgeoisie contentment. A woman, seemingly a nun, holds out to him a rosary and a prayer book. But he contentedly sleeps. Says Willimon, "This is Sloth, refusing the God-given means to make our lives interesting."[5]

THERE IS A PRESCRIPTION FOR PASSION

The big question before us, therefore, is "How do we overcome sloth?" There is a prescription for passion. In Revelation 3:18, John continues, **"I counsel you**

to buy from me gold refined in the fire, so you can become rich; and white clothes to wear, so you can cover your shameful nakedness; and salve to put on your eyes, so you can see." Jesus' counsel is to open our eyes and carry our cross. It's a call to be on fire for Jesus Christ. Think once again of the woman in Luke 7. She kissed Jesus and anointed his feet with oil. She expressed her devotion. She was passionate about Jesus. She put the religious Pharisee to shame. Where did she find or how did she get such passion? She understood and admitted her need for Jesus. And likewise we recover our passion by developing Habit #4.

HABIT # 4 – FEED YOUR HUNGER

It begins with the admission that you hunger for God. Then you can feed that hunger. Jesus said, in the Beatitudes, that blessing comes from hungering and thirsting for righteousness, for a right relationship with Jesus.

SEEK THE LORD

So develop the discipline of seeking the Lord. Like any good relationship, this takes energy and effort. Think of it this way: if you want tomatoes for your salad tonight, it will do little good to plant them in your garden this morning. It takes time for seeds to grow. And there is work that must be done to help them grow. Between the planting and the harvesting of the tomato, there must be *times of cultivating, weeding and nurturing*. That's a good picture of what it takes to develop a passion for Jesus Christ. It takes work – so work at it. Schedule time for it. Do the exercises and practice the disciplines that make for strong relationships. Church of the Savior in Washington DC has established disciplines that every member must observe in order to maintain membership. One member reflected, "Our disciplines...are that we will worship each Sunday. We will have an hour of devotion each morning. We will be in one of the mission groups of the church, engaged with the world at some place of need. And we will tithe proportionately, beginning with a tenth of our income."[6] If these disciplines were required for membership in the church you attend, would you be a member? Or if you do not attend a church, would you join one with such requirements? Perhaps you're thinking, "But that's requiring things; faith is what counts and I have faith. These things just fill more time and make me live by law, not grace." No – they are disciplines that promote growth. Listen to this person's conclusion: "As I began to practice these, my faith deepened and grew and has ever since." Growth in passion comes from seeking the Lord through disciplined cultivating, weeding, and nurturing. In an address given to ministers and workers after his ninetieth birthday, the great preacher George Mueller spoke of himself:

> "I was converted in November, 1825, but I only came into the full surrender of the heart four years later, in July, 1829. The love of

money was gone, the love of place was gone, the love of position was gone, and the love of worldly pleasures and engagements was gone. God, God alone became my portion. I found my all in Him; I wanted nothing else. And by the grace of God this has remained, and has made me a happy man, an exceedingly happy man, and it led me to care only about the things of God. I ask affectionately, my beloved brethren, have you fully surrendered the heart to God, or is there this thing or that thing with which you are taken up irrespective of God? I read a little of the Scriptures before, but preferred other books; but since that time the revelation He has made of Himself has become unspeakably blessed to me, and I can say from my heart, God is an infinitely lovely Being. Oh, be not satisfied until in your own inmost soul you can say, 'God is an infinitely lovely Being!'"[7]

Are you hungry for God? How will you feed your hunger?

SERVE THE LORD

Once you seek the Lord you can then serve the Lord. And the amazing truth is that as you serve Jesus you will come to know Him on a deeper level because you will be on the way to becoming like Him. Consider Jesus' life. Jesus did the will of His Father. In the Garden of Gethsemane He prayed that He would have the strength to do His Father's will and die on the cross. As He died on the cross, He said, **"It is finished,"** which meant He had completed what God sent Him to do. He lived what He taught, that *total surrender is the key to a passionate life*. Here's how he stated it: **"A student is not above his teacher, nor a servant above his master. It is enough for the student to be like his teacher, and the servant like his master...do not be afraid of those who kill the body but cannot kill the soul. Rather, be afraid of the one who can destroy both soul and body in hell...anyone who loves his father or mother more than me is not worthy of me; anyone who loves his son or daughter more than me is not worthy of me; and anyone who does not take his cross and follow me is not worthy of me. Whoever finds his life will lose it, and whoever loses his life for my sake will find it"** (Matthew 10:24-39).

The Apostle Paul must have caught the vision. He wrote, **"So whether you eat or drink or whatever you do, do it all for the glory of God...whatever you do, work at it with all your heart, as working for the Lord, not for men, since you know that you will receive an inheritance from the Lord as a reward. It is the Lord Jesus you are serving"** (1 Corinthians 10:31 & Colossians 3:23-24). *Work with all your heart...as for the Lord.*

So I ask you again: have you ever hunted or wished for an easier way of life? How about for an easier faith or religious life? How's your passion for the Lord? Is it hot, cold, or lukewarm – or even absent? Have the pain and pace of life begun to wear you down? Are you hungry for something more – perhaps for Jesus? So how will you feed your hunger? The Bible states: **"The eyes of the Lord run to and fro throughout the whole earth, to show himself strong in the behalf of them whose heart is perfect toward him"** (2 Chronicles 16:9). Mrs. Charles Cowman, in *Streams in the Desert,* wrote, "God is looking for a man, or woman, whose heart will be always set on Him, and who will trust Him for all He desires to do. God is eager to work more mightily now than He ever has through any soul... The world is waiting yet to see what God can do through a consecrated soul. Not the world alone, but God Himself is waiting for one, who will be more fully devoted to Him than any who have ever lived; who will be willing to be nothing that Christ may be all; who will grasp God's own purposes; and taking His humility and His faith, His love and His power, will, without hindering, continue to let God do exploits."[8]

Perhaps that's why Jesus extended an invitation to the church in Laodicea: **"Those whom I love I rebuke and discipline. So be earnest, and repent. Here I am! I stand at the door and knock. If anyone hears my voice and opens the door, I will come in and eat with him, and he with me"** (Revelation 3: 19-20). I invite you right now to come to Jesus. Release your busyness and your apathy; release your self-designed goals and purposes that are driving your life. Turn over the pain. Feed your hunger. Be the person God is waiting for!

I invite you to pray: Lord Jesus Christ – I admit I am hungry. The pain and pace of life have overwhelmed me. I am tired. And I am empty. I have often heard you knocking but I've left you standing outside. But now I have heard your voice and am opening the door of my heart. I am ready to eat with you, to love you, and to serve you. I want to be the person you're waiting for. Please, Lord Jesus, come in today; come in to stay. Amen.

7 Habits of Highly Healthy People: Aim for Simplicity
(Defeat Greed)
2 Chronicles 31:2-10 & Luke 12:13-21

Winnie-the-Pooh – the friendly but not too bright bear – went to see Rabbit, who lived in a hole in the ground. Rabbit, being a good host, offered Winnie some honey from the honey jar, only to watch in dismay as Pooh proceeded to gulp down the entire jar of honey. Then, in eat-and-run fashion, Pooh said "Good-bye" and started up the hole. But, half way up, he got stuck. Rabbit asked, "What's the matter, Pooh?" Answered Pooh, "The trouble is, Rabbit, your door is too small." Said Rabbit, "The trouble is, Pooh, you've eaten too much."

What a story of greed and its destructive nature! I wonder: how often have you grabbed for more than you've really needed? Jesus has a word of warning. In response to a young man who wanted Him to solve a dispute with his brother over their inheritance, Jesus responded with a warning against greed: **"Watch out! Be on your guard against all kinds of greed;**

a man's life does not consist in the abundance of his possessions" (Luke 12:15). He then illustrated his warning through a parable about a greedy farmer. It's important, then, that we understand more about greed!

THE CHARACTER OF GREED

So just what is the character of greed? The brother, who wanted Jesus to side with him, and the rich farmer in Jesus' parable, were both driven by a need for more. And that's the essence of greed: it is an inordinate desire for more.

AN INORDINATE DESIRE FOR MORE

It's a fondness for accumulating more just for the sake of having more – a love of money and possessions that leads to compulsive behavior. It's the 'super-size' mentality. Think, for example, of the fast food industry. In its early years, there was only one size of everything. Now the original French fry serving size is the 'small' size and there are medium, large, and super-size quantities. That original size is still here, at about 200 calories, while the super size weighs in at over 600 calories. At its opening, Burger King had two drink sizes, a 12-ounce small and a 16-ounce large. But today, the 12-ounce is for kids, the 16-ounce is now the small, the medium is 32 ounces, and the biggest is 42 ounces. Over the years auto manufacturers have enlarged car cup holders to accommodate the Double Gulp-sized soft drink cups that contain 64 ounces (that's half a gallon of soda) containing between 600-800 calories.[1] These fast food restaurant portions are a potent metaphor for greed. The more we get, even if we pay a little more, even if it's not good for us, the more we want – and there is no such thing as enough.

MANIFESTS ITSELF IN SEVERAL WAYS

This inordinate desire for more manifests itself in several ways.

First, *it drives people to become excessively thrifty*. They become tight-fisted, stingy, and hate to give anything away. Thus they develop callousness towards the needy and even towards the rich. The greedy person loathes paying off debt and will try to avoid doing so.

Second, a counterpart to this is *a tendency to be excessively profit oriented*. A greedy person often becomes a workaholic, a cutthroat competitor, even a swindler or miser. He or she loves the get-rich-quick schemes. They will, for example, spend a lot of time entering all the contests and giveaways. In the extreme cases they are prone to excessive interest in, or even addiction to gambling. Greed's profit orientation also includes hoarding, storing away, and keeping for the sake of keeping, even if the items are no longer useable or practical.

And, third, both of these excesses indicate that greedy persons, at their core, *lack trust in God* to provide for their daily needs. They have not taken to heart Jesus' words: **"Do not store up for yourselves**

treasures on earth where moth and rust destroy... do not worry about your life, what you will eat or drink; or about your body, what you will wear...O you of little faith...all these things will be given to you...Therefore do not worry about tomorrow..." (Mt. 6:19 ff.).

Is it any wonder Jesus spoke more about money and possessions than any other topic? And His message must have gotten through to some of his closest followers. James, in a letter he wrote to the early church, said: **"What causes fights and quarrels among you? Don't they come from your desires that battle within you? You want something but don't get it. You kill and covet, but you cannot have what you want. You quarrel and fight. You do not have, because you do not ask God. When you ask, you do not receive, because you ask with wrong motives, that you may spend what you get on your pleasures"** (James 4:1-3). Greed is at the core of our fights and quarrels, and even a reason for unanswered prayer.

BASIC CAUSES OF GREED

So how do people become greedy? How do you and I become greedy? What are some basic causes of greed?

THREE COMMON MISCONCEPTIONS ABOUT POSSESSIONS

One cause is that there are three common misconceptions about possessions. One such misconception is that *having more will make me happier*. "If only I had more money, a bigger car, more house, more clothes..." Think about it – the more you own, the more space, repairs and maintenance will be needed; there will be more requests from others for money and donations necessitating still more time and money. Many adults today have more than their parents ever had yet are enjoying it less and are deeper in debt. They live on a treadmill trying to keep up and get ahead. It's like trying to fill the Grand Canyon with marbles – it will never happen. There just aren't enough marbles. Having more will not make us happier. Rather, the reality is that it's like drinking salt water when you're thirsty – the more you drink the thirstier you will become.

Andrew Carnegie was born in poverty and grew to become one of the wealthiest persons of his time. In later years, reflecting on his life, he said that he would not exchange the sacred memories of his humble home with the richest millionaire's son who ever breathed. "I would as soon leave to my son a curse as the almighty dollar...Millionaires seldom smile."[2] Did having more make him happier? American industrialist and philanthropist John D. Rockefeller said, "I have made many millions, but they have brought me no happiness."[3] Did having more make him happier?

No wonder the wise preacher of Ecclesiastes wrote: **"Whoever loves money never has money enough; whoever loves wealth is never satisfied with his income. This too is meaningless. As goods increase, so do those who consume them. And what benefit are they to the owner except to feast his eyes on them?"** (Ecclesiastes 5:10-11). Or as the New Living Translation puts it: **"Those who love money will never have enough. How absurd to think that wealth brings true happiness! The more you have, the more people come to help you spend it. So what is the advantage of wealth-except perhaps to watch it run through your fingers?"**

A second misconception is that *having more will increase my worth*. Yet in reality, greed is buying things with money we do not have to impress people we do not know or like. Why? Because we tend to think our net-worth is the same as our self-worth. Back in 1923, a very important meeting was held at the Edgewater Beach Hotel in Chicago. In attendance were nine of the world's most successful financiers: the president of the largest independent steel company, the president of the largest gas company, the largest wheat speculator, the president of the New York Stock Exchange, a member of the President's cabinet, the greatest 'bear' on Wall Street, the head of the world's largest monopoly, and the president of the Bank of International Settlements. These men had certainly learned the formula for financial success. Did having more make them happy? The president of the world's largest independent steel company – Charles Schwab – died bankrupt and lived on borrowed money for five years before his death. The president of the greatest utility company – Samuel Insull – died a fugitive from justice and penniless in a foreign country. The president of the largest gas company – Howard Hopson – became insane. The greatest wheat speculator – Arthur Cutten – died abroad, insolvent or bankrupt. The president of the New York Stock Exchange – Richard Whitney – served an extended sentence in Sing Sing. The member of the President's cabinet – Albert Fall – was pardoned from prison so that he could die at home. The greatest 'bear' of Wall Street – Jesse Livermore – committed suicide. The head of the world's greatest monopoly – Ivan Krueger – committed suicide.[4] Did having more make them happier or increase their worth?

That's why Jesus said: "…**a man's life does not consist in the abundance of his possessions**" (Luke 12:15). You are not what you own! You are what – or who – owns you! Who or what owns you? Can you say with conviction that you are not your own but belong, body and soul, to your faithful Savior Jesus Christ?[3] There's your net worth.

The third misconception is *having more will give me more security*. Of course, that security disappears as soon as the stock market turns down and insurance rates go up! Solomon, in Proverbs, wrote: **"Whoever trusts in his riches will fall, but the righteous will thrive like a green leaf"** (11:28). A fisherman was sitting lazily beside his boat when a well-dressed businessman stopped by. The businessman was disturbed that the fisherman was lying idly on the bank, so asked why he was not out in the river catching fish.

The fisherman replied, "I've caught enough fish for today." Said the businessman, "Why don't you catch more fish than you need?" "Why would I want to do that?" asked the fisherman. "You could make more money, buy a bigger boat, go deeper, and catch even more fish. Pretty soon, you would be rich and have a fleet of boats like me," replied the businessman. "Then what would I do?" the fisherman asked. Answered the rich businessman, "You could sit and enjoy life." Replied the fisherman, "What do you think I am doing now?" He understood that security is internal, not external. As Jesus said: **"Look at the birds of the air; they do not sow or reap or store away in barns, and yet your heavenly father feeds them. Are you not much more valuable than they? ...Therefore do not worry about tomorrow, for tomorrow will worry about itself"** (Mt. 6:34). Does having more make you happier, increase your worth, or give you more security?

THREE COMMON MISTAKES CONCERNING POSSESSIONS

There are also three common mistakes concerning possessions that cause greed to creep into our lives. In the parable the young man queried to himself, **"You have plenty of good things laid up for many years. Take life easy..."** (Luke12:19). But God countered, **"You fool! This very night..."**

The young man was a fool, said Jesus, because his first mistake was to *assume longevity over brevity*. James 4:13-15 similarly cautions: **"Now listen, you** who say, 'today or tomorrow we will go to this or that city, spend a year there, carry on business and make money.' Why, you do not even know what will happen tomorrow. What is your life? You are a mist that appears for a little while and then vanishes. Instead, you ought to say, 'If it is the lord's will, we will live and do this or that.'" Do you know when you are going to die? Greed vanishes when we consider the brevity of life.

A second mistake for the young fool was to *value the body over the soul*. The fool bragged, **"Take life easy; eat, drink, and be merry."** But God replied, **"This very night your life will be demanded of you."** We live in an age when care for the body is deemed more important than care for the soul. Imagine what would happen if more people spent the time used in gyms, workouts and diets working instead on their relationship with Jesus Christ? What would happen if the money spent on these efforts was used instead for the Kingdom of God? Immediately after the parable, Jesus said:

> **"Therefore I tell you, do not worry about your life, what you will eat; or about your body, what you will wear. Life is more than food, and the body more than clothes. Consider the ravens: they do not sow or reap, they have no storeroom or barn; yet God feeds them. And how much more valuable you are than birds! Who of you by worrying can add a single hour to his life? Since you cannot do this very little**

thing, why do you worry about the rest? "Consider how the lilies grow. They do not labor or spin. Yet I tell you, not even Solomon in all his splendor was dressed like one of these. If that is how God clothes the grass of the field, which is here today, and tomorrow is thrown into the fire, how much more will he clothe you, O you of little faith! And do not set your heart on what you will eat or drink; do not worry about it. For the pagan world runs after all such things, and your Father knows that you need them. But seek his kingdom, and these things will be given to you as well" (Luke 12:22-31).

The fool's third mistake about possessions was *claiming ownership of what belongs to God.* The fool said, **"I will tear down my barns and build bigger ones, and there I will store all my grain and my goods. And I'll say to myself, 'You have plenty of good things laid up for many years.'"** God responded, **"This very night your life will be demanded from you. Then who will get what you have prepared for yourself?"** It's an issue of ownership – who really owns it all? Aristotle Onassis, a wealthy Greek ship owner and financier, lamented, "I've just been a machine for making money. I seem to have spent my life in a golden tunnel looking for the outlet which would lead to happiness. But the tunnel kept going on. After my death there will be nothing left."[5] Who really owns it all?

HABIT #5 – AIM FOR SIMPLICITY – THE CURE FOR GREED

So what's the cure for greed? Put most succinctly, aim for and develop the habit of simplicity. Jesus, still speaking after sharing the parable (Luke 12:34) said, **"Where your treasure is, there your heart will be also."**

FOCUS ON GODLY TREASURES

The key is to focus on godly treasures. To do so, first, *de-accumulate your possessions.* I'm not saying we all need to give everything away and adopt a poverty level of living. I am saying, along with Jesus, we need to evaluate our priorities. As a pastor friend of mine once said, "It's not the high cost of living that's the problem, it's the cost of high living."[6] As the philosopher Epicures wrote, "Wealth consists not in having great possessions but in having few wants."[7] Rabbi Simeon reflected, "I have never seen a stag as a dryer of figs, or a lion as a porter, or a fox as a merchant, yet they are all nourished without worry. If they, who are created to serve me, are nourished without worry, how much more ought I, who am created to serve my Maker, to be nourished without worry; but I have corrupted my ways, and so I have impaired my substance."[8] Trim away the excess. Get rid of the clutter. Hebrews 12:1 is very clear: **"...let us throw off everything that hinders and the sin that so easily entangles, and run with perseverance the race marked out for us."** See the point?

Runners have no weights – no clutter – as they run! De-accumulate your possessions.

A second step in the cure for greed is to *discipline spending*. Make sure your income matches, or exceeds, your outgo. Work at getting out of debt. Say no to buy-now- pay-later. Buy only what you need and can afford. The great Albert Schweitzer, a medical missionary, had a standard wardrobe. He wore a white pith helmet, white shirt and pants, and a black tie. He had worn the hat for forty years and the tie for twenty. Someone told him one day that some men owned dozens of neckties; Schweitzer remarked, *"For one neck?"*[9] Discipline your spending. Make sure your outgo doesn't exceed your income.

The third and one of the best cures for greed is to *develop a giving lifestyle*. In 2nd Chronicles 31:2-10 we are told that King Hezekiah...

"...ordered the people living in Jerusalem to give the portion due the priests and Levites so they could devote themselves to the Law of the LORD. As soon as the order went out, the Israelites generously gave the first fruits of their grain, new wine, oil and honey and all that the fields produced. They brought a great amount, a tithe of everything...Since the people began to bring their contributions to the temple of the LORD, we have had enough to eat and plenty to spare, because the LORD has blessed his people, and this great amount is left over." In our Luke passage, Jesus continued: **"Sell your possessions and give to the poor. Provide purses for yourselves that will not wear out, a treasure in heaven that will not be exhausted, where no thief comes near and no moth destroys. For where your treasure is, there your heart will be also"** (vss.33-34).

A fourth step for greed, and the most significant, is to *deepen your trust in Jesus.* Take Him at His word. If you hold on to Jesus you cannot hold on to the things of the earth. Only when you believe that Jesus' word is faithful and true and that His riches are inexhaustible and never failing will you be able to overcome the temptation of greed and live a simpler life. So one more time, hear the Word of our Lord: **"Do not store up for yourselves treasures on earth where moth and rust destroy...do not worry about your life, what you will eat or drink; or about your body, what you will wear...O you of little faith...all these things will be given to you...therefore do not worry about tomorrow..."**

As a hymn, these words of Anna Olander are not very well known. Yet, based on Luke 9:25, **"What good is it for a man to gain the whole world, and**

yet lose or forfeit his very self?" her words are a fitting testimony.

"If I Gained the World."

"If I gained the world, but lost the Savior, were my
life worth living for a day?
Could my yearning heart find rest and comfort in
the things that soon must pass away?
If I gained the world, but lost the Savior; would my
gain be worth the life-long strife?
Are all the earthly pleasures worth comparing for a
moment with a Christ-filled life?

Had I wealth and love in fullest measure, and a
name revered both far and near,
Yet no hope beyond, no harbor waiting where my
storm-tossed vessel I could steer –
If I gained the world, but lost the Savior who
endured the cross and died for me,
Could then all the world afford a refuge whither in
my anguish I might flee?

O what emptiness without the Savior mid the sins
and sorrows here below!
And eternity, how dark without Him – only night
and tears and endless woe!
What tho I might live without the Savior, when I
come to die, how would it be?
O to face the valley's gloom without Him! And
without Him all eternity!

O the joy of having all in Jesus! What a balm the broken heart to heal!
Ne'er a sin so great but He'll forgive it, nor a sorrow that He does not feel!
If I have but Jesus, only Jesus, Nothing else in all the world beside,
O then everything is mine in Jesus – for my needs and more He will provide."[10]

It is my sincere prayer that you will gain the Savior as you aim for simplicity.

7 Habits of Highly Healthy People: Guard your Mind
(Defeat Lust)
2 Samuel 11:1-27

The Illinois Department of Natural Resources reported that more than 17,000 deer die each year after being struck by motorists on their state highways. The peak season for road kills is late fall. Why? Because in November, according to the state wildlife director, "They're concentrating almost exclusively on reproductive activities and are a lot less wary than they normally would be."[1] The book of Samuel, by honestly portraying King David's life, reminds us that deer aren't the only ones destroyed by preoccupation with sex. It certainly isn't surprising that lust is one of the seven deadly sins.

THE PROPERTIES OF LUST

Much has been written, especially in recent years, about the properties of lust – far more than I can incorporate in this chapter. So I will emphasize and clarify two properties of lust.

THE POWER OF LUST

Lust can be defined as, "to luxuriate, to soak in what is impure; gratification without giving." Lust does not appreciate another person's beauty, but desires, fantasizes about and makes plans for it. As such it is a self-centered drive that seeks to fulfill its own desires without concern for the desires of another. Lust is a controlling yearning or longing, a *passionate, overmastering desire – not limited to but primarily sexual*. For example, consider David. It was not just a case of being enraptured by Bathsheba's beauty. He "luxuriated and wanted to soak in what was impure." From the moment he saw her he desired, fantasized and planned – he thought only of fulfilling his own desires. And that passion mastered and drove him.

THE PATTERNS OF LUST

Not only are the passions and drive of lust strong and overwhelming but there are also some distinctive patterns of lust. Studies convincingly show that lust *leads to all manner of sexual sin and immorality*. It inevitably ends up in adultery (sexual relationships where at least one person is married to someone other than the sexual partner), fornication (sex where neither party is married), pornography, perverted sex acts (same gender sex, pedophilia, bestiality, sadism, masochism, voyeurism, exhibitionism – and if you're not sure of what all of these are, it's a good thing!), or fantasizing any of this. Additionally lust fosters promiscuity, rape, incest, prostitution, unhappy marriages, divorce, bitterness, guilt, disillusionment, and unhealthy relationships.

I said that this pattern is inevitable. I base my opinion not only on research, but also on the fact that *there is a very definite slippery slope.* The more attention and energy a person devotes to sexual matters, the less attention and energy he or she spends on spiritual things, such as building a relationship with Jesus Christ. When we let go of the spiritual things of life, when we begin to live less for God, we start living only for ourselves. Then the demands of the flesh increase.

But that's not all. The slope continues. *The more we sin, the less we think about sin.* Isn't that what we're experiencing in America? Immoral sexual relationships, as long as they are consensual, have now become acceptable as instruments for pleasure, apart from any commitment. On an episode of the ABC television talk show "Politically Incorrect," (2-15-01) host Bill Maher was discussing some rules for relationships from the male perspective. In regard to sex he said, "Don't [gripe] about porn." When the panel (three of whom were women) asked what he meant, he responded, "Unless you [women] are willing to give us sex whenever we want, you don't have the right to gripe if we use pornography." Surprisingly, all three women agreed that the rule made sense.[2] This rule and response demonstrate the distorted attitude towards sexuality prevalent in our society.

Sex is seen as primarily for one's personal physical pleasure, and whatever is for one's personal pleasure is okay. It has become acceptable because there is no sense of sin and therefore no sense of shame. Dr. William Backus, an ordained clergyman and founder of the Center for Christian Psychological Services, wrote, "...it moves quickly from unthinkable to thinkable to interesting to acceptable and finally from acceptable to codification into law."[3] Persecution and ridicule await those of us who faithfully proclaim the biblical, moral view. Society tries to silence us so there will be no sense of shame and wrong.

THE PATH OF LUST

Since lust is so powerful, and the slope so slippery, it's important to be sensitive to the path it takes. It is critical to identify how our decisions and actions put us either firmly on the slope or keep us off it. This is where the story of King David is so instructive. David's decisions and actions put him firmly on the slope.

DAVID FAILED TO KEEP HIS HABITS

First of all, David failed to keep his habits. David was ignoring his basic responsibilities. Verse 1: **"In the spring, at the time when kings go off to war, David sent Joab out with the king's men and the whole Israelite army."** David was in the wrong place – he should have been with the army, but he stayed home. He had changed his life long habit. Throughout the years he had stayed busy with his armies and kept active throughout the days. It's been stated succinctly, "He had kept his hands clean, because he had kept them busy."² When he was no longer busy, when he had changed his good habits, he had time on his hands – and with time on his hands he had less focus and wandered away from his normal boundaries of life. He failed to recognize that the habits which had kept him active in healthy ways, also kept him from sin. We become vulnerable when we have too much unstructured time on our hands and therefore less focus to our lives.

HE FAILED TO KEEP HIS EYES UNDER CONTROL

With more time and less focus, David's next step down the path of lust was that he failed to keep his eyes under control. He was not only in the wrong place physically; he was in the wrong place mentally and spiritually. *He longed to look and looked too long.* There's an old adage that adultery – and I would add lust – starts in the head before it reaches the bed. Satan gets into our sight, then into our feelings, and then urges us to action. Isn't this the same process advertisers use? Why do companies spend so much money on advertising? And why do they try so hard to get us to look at their ads? They know that if they get into our eyes they will arouse and penetrate our feelings – and once they arouse and penetrate our feelings we will act. Why is it that television and movie producers show more and more skin and sex?

Because they know that if they get into our eyes they will arouse and penetrate our feelings – and once they arouse and penetrate our feelings they will get our attention and action. It's no wonder that in his intense suffering Job proclaimed **"I made a covenant with my eyes not to look lustfully at a girl"** (31:1). I still remember the song I often sang as a small child: "Oh be careful little eyes what you see…" I sang it innocently then – now I understand it's deep truth and must sing it with utmost conviction. After all, Jesus said **"…I tell you that anyone who looks at a woman lustfully has already committed adultery with her in his heart. If your right eye causes you to sin, gouge it out and throw it away. It is better for you to lose one part of your body than for your whole body to be thrown into hell"** (Matthew 5:28-29). Keep your eyes under control!

HE WALKED IN THE WRONG DIRECTION

With more time and less focus, with his eyes out of control, David then walked in the wrong direction. David made a commitment to act out his fantasy by fulfilling his desires; he asked for Bathsheba to be brought to him. 2nd Samuel 11 tells the rest of the sad, sordid story. But can you see what happens? *Once we get close to, and touch and feel the object of our lust, we're doomed.* Isn't that why the car salesman lets you test-drive the car? Isn't that why stores and manufacturers allow you to try a product with the promise that you can return it if you're not satisfied? Once we've gotten close to something, it's hard to part with it. David could have turned his head and walked away – but he walked in the wrong direction.

HE EXPERIENCED A CHAIN OF BAD STEPS AND EVENTS

Because he walked in the wrong direction, David experienced a chain of bad steps and events. He committed murder, his family experienced rape, rebellion and murder, and it all caused the death of his own son. The biblical message is very clear: *When we cross God's boundaries there will be consequences.* We don't break God's laws – they break us. In physics the law is stated this way: for every action there is an equal and opposite reaction. **"Can a man scoop fire into his lap without his clothes being burned? Can a man walk on hot coals without his feet being scorched"** (Proverbs 6:27-28)?

THE PATH FROM LUST

If lust is part of your life, read these next words carefully and prayerfully. There is always forgiveness. To turn away, begin here. Before you do anything else, ask God for forgiveness. And claim the promise that **"If we confess our sins, he is faithful and just and will forgive us our sins and purify us from all unrighteousness"** (I John 1:9). Then you can follow the path from lust. And you don't have to walk the path alone. The Bible assures us, **"It is God's will that you should be sanctified: that you should avoid sexual immorality; that each of you should learn** to control his own body in a way that is holy and honorable, not in passionate lust like the heathen, who do not know God..." (1 Thessalonians 4:3-5).

HABIT #6 – GUARD YOUR MIND – DEFEAT LUST

What is the way to avoid immorality? Practice Habit #6 – guard your mind. How can you do that?

MINIMIZE OPPORTUNITIES FOR LUST

First, minimize opportunities for lust. **"Your eye is the lamp of your body. When your eyes are good, your whole body also is full of light. But when they are bad, your body also is full of darkness. See to it, then, that the light within you is not darkness"** (Luke 11:34-35). In other words, avoid tempting situations. A transport company placed an ad that read, "Wanted: Conscientious and experienced truck driver to transport TNT across narrow mountain roads. Pay is very good." The foreman asked each applicant this question: "When you round a curve on a tight mountain road, how close to the edge can you drive without slipping off?" The first applicant responded, "Oh, I've had years of experience at that! I can get as close as a foot from the edge." The second one said, "I can hang the outside edge of my tire over the edge and still stay on the road." The third stated, "I respect the load and the danger. I would never get close enough to find out." Guess who got the job! The moral is obvious: don't get too close to the edge! In other words, don't watch films and videos that tempt your eyes. Turn off the TV. Stay off the porn Internet sites (There are more than 1.5 million sites![4]). Don't listen to the music groups that push the rhythm or sing the words that tempt you. Move your computer into a room where there are other people who will be watching you. Quit your job. Avoid certain people; alter your social life. *Get away from temptation, no matter what it costs.* It's been said that we are not responsible for the first look, but we are for the second one! For example, here's how the young ruler Joseph handled sexual temptation:

> **"From the time he put him in charge of his household and of all that he owned, the LORD blessed the household of the Egyptian because of Joseph. The blessing of the LORD was on everything Potiphar had, both in the house and in the field. So he left in Joseph's care everything he had; with Joseph in charge, he did not concern himself with anything except the food he ate. Now Joseph was well built and handsome, and after a while his master's wife took notice of Joseph and said, 'Come to bed with me!' But he refused. 'With me in charge,' he told her, 'my master does not concern himself with anything in the house; everything he owns he has entrusted to my care. No one is greater in this house than I am. My master has withheld nothing from me except you, because you are his wife.**

How then could I do such a wicked thing and sin against God?' And though she spoke to Joseph day after day, he refused to go to bed with her or even be with her. One day he went into the house to attend to his duties, and none of the household servants was inside. She caught him by his cloak and said, 'Come to bed with me!' But he left his cloak in her hand and ran out of the house" (Genesis 39:5-6).

The Apostle Paul put it very succinctly: **"Flee from sexual immorality"** (1 Corinthians 6:18.).

MAINTAIN YOUR PLACE

Second, as you minimize your opportunities, maintain your place. Once you get into the right place, keep walking the right path. A good way to do this is to *build accountability into your life*. If you need counseling, go get it. If you need a group of friends to work with you, ask them. Do not try to go it alone. Former NBA star A. C. Green is an outstanding example.[5] Green's faith and moral stand was no secret to his teammates. "They respected me and were curious about how I [remain abstinent]. They asked me privately or threw questions at me in the locker room." In *Sports Illustrated,* columnist Rick Reilly dubbed Green "The NBA Player Who Has Never Scored." Green admits that he's not immune from sexual temptation. But he maintains his integrity with the help of friends in Champions for Christ and others who keep him accountable and focused on his godly commitment. "They keep me in line so much that I'm sure there have been temptations waiting around the corner that thankfully I've never known about." As Green told Reilly, "I promised God this, and I'm not going to break it. I love myself and my future wife too much to just waste it." His actions don't go unnoticed. Teammate Anthony Mason, who had off-court troubles, began to pay attention to Green's spiritual leadership. In the *Miami Herald* Mason said, "You would think of Green as a goody-two-shoes, but to see [his convictions] up close, you realize that's the way you're supposed to live." Green has had the thrill of leading teammates to Christ, but even more often he has helped them work through specific issues in their lives. And, even in retirement, he's always been available to pray. Maintain your place. Stay on the right path.

MONITOR YOUR THOUGHTS

A good aid to help with this maintenance is to monitor your thoughts. Perhaps you've heard it said, "Garbage in, garbage out." What goes into our minds is what works itself out in our lives. Consider Schopenhauer's Law of Entropy: "If you put a spoonful of wine in a barrel full of sewage you get sewage. If you put a spoonful of sewage in a barrel of wine, you get sewage." *So stay away from the sewage.* J. Oswald Sanders put it, " The mind of man is the battleground on which every moral and spiritual battle is fought."[6] Leslie Flynn is even more explicit: "Every kidnapping was once a thought. Every extramarital affair was first a fantasy."[7] A great place to begin monitoring your thoughts is to attend worship faithfully. Put yourself in the good environment. Isn't it amazing that some people wouldn't think of missing a day of work, but often don't think twice about missing a service of worship? Don't miss! And get a good, daily 'brain cleansing' – immerse yourself in God's Word. I was deeply influenced the first time I read this line: "The best way to break free from sin is to whet your appetite for something different." It's really what the apostle Paul meant when he wrote, **"...we take captive every thought to make it obedient to Christ"** (2 Corinthians 10:5). And here's his guideline for how to do so: **"Finally, brothers, whatever is true, whatever is noble, whatever is right, whatever is pure, whatever is lovely, whatever is admirable— if anything is excellent or praiseworthy—think about such things"** (Phil. 4:8). **"Therefore, prepare your minds for action; be self-controlled; set your hope fully on the grace to be given you when Jesus Christ is revealed. As obedient children, do not conform to the evil desires you had when you lived in ignorance. But just as he who called you is holy, so be holy in all you do..."** (1 Pt. 1:13-15). Whet your appetite for something different! What a great way to monitor your thoughts!

So I want to whet your appetite for Jesus. Let these words of author and pastor John Piper instruct you.

"We must not give a sexual image or impulse more than five seconds before we mount a violent counterattack with the mind. I mean that! Five seconds. In the first two seconds we shout, '<u>No! Get out of my head!</u>' In the next two seconds we cry out: '<u>O God, in the name of Jesus, help me. Save me now. I am yours.</u>' Good beginning. But then the real battle begins. This is a mind war. The absolute necessity is to get the image and the impulse out of our mind. How? Get a counter-image into the mind. Fight. Push. Strike. Don't ease up. It must be an image that is so powerful that the other image cannot survive. There are lust-destroying images and thoughts. For example, have you ever in the first five seconds of temptation, demanded of your mind that it look steadfastly at the crucified form of Jesus Christ? Picture this. You have just seen a peek-a-boo blouse inviting further fantasy. You have five seconds. '<u>No! Get out of my mind! God help me!</u>' Now, immediately, demand of your mind—you can do this by the Spirit (Romans 8:13). Demand of your mind to fix its gaze on Christ on the cross. Use all your fantasizing power to see his lacerated back. Thirty-nine lashes left little flesh intact. He heaves with his breath up and down against the rough vertical beam of the cross. Each breath puts splinters into the lacerations. The Lord gasps. From time to time he screams out with intolerable pain. He tries to pull away from the wood and the massive spikes though his wrists rip into the nerve endings and he screams again with agony and pushes up with his feet to give some relief to his wrists. But the bones and nerves in his pierced feet crush against each other with anguish and he screams again. There is no relief. His throat is raw from screaming and thirst. He loses his breath and thinks he is suffocating, and suddenly his body involuntarily gasps for air and all the injuries unite in pain. In torment, he forgets about the crown of two-inch thorns and throws his head back in desperation, only to hit one of the thorns perpendicular against the cross beam and drive it half an inch into his skull. His voice reaches a soprano pitch of pain and sobs break over his pain-wracked body as every cry brings more and more pain. Now, I am not thinking about the blouse any more. I am at Calvary."[8]

And so are we.

> "See from His head, His hands, His feet,
> Sorrow and love flow mingled down;
> Did e'er such love and sorrow meet,
> Or thorns compose so rich a crown?
>
> Were the whole realm of nature mine,
> That were a present far too small:
> Love so amazing, so divine,
> Demands my soul, my life, my all."[9]

If you struggle with lust, even just slightly, I encourage you to pray right now: Lord Jesus, guard my mind. Help me stay away from the sewage. Help me flee the temptation that is reeling me into the land of sin. Show me the person you've appointed to hold me accountable and give me the courage to ask them to do so. Help me to think about **"...whatever is true, whatever is noble, whatever is right, whatever is pure, whatever is lovely, whatever is admirable, and whatever is excellent or praiseworthy."** Help me to set my hope and sight on your grace. Lord Jesus, I need you. Help me claim victory. In the strength and power of your name, I pray. Amen.

7 Habits of Highly Healthy People: Restrain Yourself
(Defeat Gluttony)
Ephesians 5:1-20

In *The Lion, the Witch and the Wardrobe*, Edmund Pevensie loves Turkish Delight. Jadis, the White Witch, meets Edmund in some snow-filled woods and exploits his weakness by offering him a warm drink and Turkish Delight. From the first bite, he is hooked, for each "piece was sweet and light to the very centre and Edmund had never tasted anything more delicious." Jadis repeatedly offers him more Delight in exchange for more information regarding the whereabouts of his brother and sisters. Driven by an insatiable hunger for more and more Turkish Delight Edmund readily responds: "At first Edmund tried to remember that it is rude to speak with one's mouth full, but soon he forgot about this and thought only of trying to shovel down as much Turkish Delight as he could, and the more he ate, the more he wanted to eat, and he never asked himself why the Queen should be so inquisitive."[1] The whole scene personifies gluttony, the sin of making one's belly the god one serves (Philippians 3:19). And Edmund's gluttonous desire has deadly ramifications. While Edmund is eventually saved by the intervention and intercession of Aslan – the Christ figure – the cost is deadly to Aslan. Lewis's point in emphasizing Edmund's gluttony is to illustrate vividly the effects of sins in general and this sin in particular. Overindulgence – gluttony – blinds us to the truth, turning us inward, making us slaves to our own insatiable desires.

THE DEFINITIONS OF GLUTTONY

A good place to begin is to reflect on the definitions of gluttony. Most of us associate gluttony with food, and that is part of the most common definition.

EATING EXCESSIVELY

The first definition in the dictionary is eating excessively. Certainly this is a problem that is not unfamiliar to us. One-third of all Americans (approximately sixty-three million) are overweight. Two hundred fifty thousand deaths each year are attributed to poor diet and lack of activity. Fifty percent of cardiovascular disease is related to excess weight. Americans spend as much as fifty billion dollars a year dieting – fifty billion is more than we spend on education, training, employment, and social services. We spend more on dieting than the gross national product of Ireland. Please take note: this definition of gluttony does not say that being overweight is a sin. Rather it points to excessive eating – which includes careless eating.

Did you know that on March 10, 2004, the U.S. House of Representatives passed a measure known as the "cheeseburger bill"? The bill was designed to protect the fast food industry from potential lawsuits filed by overweight customers. Caesar Barber, 56, pointed the finger at McDonald's, Wendy's, Kentucky Fried Chicken, and Burger King for his two heart attacks, diabetes, and weight problem. Gregory Rhymes, a 15-year-old high school student, joined his mother in blaming fast food restaurants for his obesity. Rhymes's mother stood before a judge and stated she "always believed McDonald's was healthy for my son." Gregory weighs nearly 400 pounds. The purpose of the "cheeseburger bill" is to stop these kinds of lawsuits. As Representative F. James Sensenbrenner Jr. said, "Don't run off and file a lawsuit...Look in the mirror because you're the one to blame."[2]

Perhaps it sounds like it's someone else's problem. But do a little self-quiz. Have you ever eaten so much that all you felt like doing was lying around? Do you often think of eating between meals? Is it easy for you to enjoy rich and tasty desserts even after you know you have eaten enough and are full? Do you spend a lot of time being concerned about your weight? Do you spend more money on alcoholic beverages than you give to Kingdom work? Are you finicky or choosy about food or drink? A "yes" answer to any of these may indicate that gluttony is your problem as well.

OVER CONSUMPTION OR OVERINDULGENCE OF ANYTHING

But gluttony can also involve things other than food. A second definition is over consumption or overindulgence of anything. Rick Ezell stated it well: "It is not about overeating on Thanksgiving. Gluttony is not about appearance; it is an attitude; it is not about being overweight; it is overindulgence. It is not about recreational eating; it is rampant excess. It is not about too many external effects; it is a lack of internal balance."[3] It's taking more than is necessary, or too much of a good thing. So people are gluttons for work, for punishment, for criticism or praise or attention, for possessions, for sexual pleasure – and for so much more.

ANY APPETITE NOT RESTRAINED; MISDIRECTED HUNGER

A third definition of gluttony is any appetite not restrained; misdirected hunger. As Bishop Fulton Sheen described it, "...it is the excess of luxury... When (people) forget their souls, they begin to take great care of their bodies. There are more athletic clubs ... than there are spiritual retreat houses; and who shall count the millions spent in beauty shops to glorify faces that will one day be the prey of worms. It is not particularly difficult to find thousands who will spend two or three hours a day in exercising, but if you ask them to bend their knees to God in five minutes of prayer they protest that it is too long."[4]

THE DANGER OF GLUTTONY

But what's the problem with gluttony? If you want to be unrestrained and overindulge, what's the big deal? We need to be aware of the danger and destructiveness of gluttony.

IT HURTS THE GLUTTON

Gluttons hurt themselves. They damage their bodies, their emotional stability, and their souls. It's like the memorable Aesop fable. A number of flies were attracted to a jar of honey that had been overturned in a housekeeper's room. Placing their feet in it, they ate greedily. Their feet, however, became so smeared with the honey that they could not use their wings, nor release themselves, and they were suffocated. Just as they were expiring, they exclaimed, "O foolish creatures that we are, for the sake of a little pleasure we have destroyed ourselves."[5]

IT HURTS OTHERS

Gluttons also hurt others. Dr. Robin Meyers pointed out, "While much of the world is starving, Americans are eating themselves to death..."[6] He added that many "Americans claim to be overtaxed and underpaid and claim that's why school children go to school without textbooks; yet our national restaurant tab could fund them for a decade."[7] The reality is that whenever we have too much of a good thing, it is always at the expense of another. And make no mistake about it – we sin whenever we consume too much at the expense of another. Over-consumption of petroleum, energy, or any natural resource is therefore no different than over-consumption of food.

IT REVEALS OUR ATTITUDE

So gluttony hurts both the glutton and others. The truth is that, at its very core, gluttony reveals our attitude towards ourselves and others. *Gluttony is not primarily about the size of our belts, but about the state of our hearts.* Jesus told a story about the rich man who had a beggar, named Lazarus, at his gate:

> **"There was a rich man who was dressed in purple and fine linen and lived in luxury every day. At his gate was laid a beggar named Lazarus, covered with sores and longing to eat what fell from the rich man's table. Even the dogs came and licked his sores. The time came when the beggar died and the angels carried him to Abraham's side. The rich man also died and was buried. In hell, where he was in torment, he looked up and saw Abraham far away, with Lazarus by his side. So he called to him, 'Father Abraham, have pity on me and send Lazarus to dip the tip of his finger in water and cool my tongue, because I am in agony in this fire.' But Abraham replied, 'Son, remember that in your lifetime you received your good**

things, while Lazarus received bad things, but now he is comforted here and you are in agony. And besides all this, between us and you a great chasm has been fixed, so that those who want to go from here to you cannot, nor can anyone cross over from there to us'" (Luke 16:19-26).

The beggar suffered daily while Lazarus lived in gluttonous luxury. He hurt the beggar. (Note that in the end, however, he hurt himself eternally.) Gluttony is not primarily about the size of our belts, but about the state of our hearts.

THE DEFEAT OF GLUTTONY

So how do we defeat gluttony? How do we get our hearts right? We restrain ourselves.

HABIT #7 – RESTRAIN YOURSELF

Paul wrote: **"It is God's will that you should be sanctified...that each of you should learn to control his own body in a way that is holy and honorable..."** (1 Thessalonians 4:4).

RESTRAINT BEGINS WITH THE BODY

"Therefore, I urge you, brothers, in view of God's mercy, to offer your bodies as living sacrifices, holy and pleasing to God—this is your spiritual act of worship" (Romans 12:1). It begins with the body because *the body houses the Holy Spirit.* **"Do you not know that your body is a temple of the Holy Spirit, who is in you, whom you have received from God? You are not your own; you were bought at a price. Therefore honor God with your body"** (1 Corinthians 6:19-20).

To discipline our bodies we need to understand that *our thoughts are critical.* **"We demolish arguments and every pretension that sets itself up against the knowledge of God, and we take captive every thought to make it obedient to Christ"** (2 Corinthians 10:5). Our minds are mental greenhouses in which the seeds of our actions grow. The religious magazine *Discipleship Journal* once had its readers rank areas of their greatest spiritual challenges. It's significant that of the top eight results, seven concerned the very deadly sins we've been considering in this book. But even more to the point is that 81% of the respondents noted that the temptations were more potent when they had neglected their time with God, and 84% said that resisting temptation was best accomplished through prayer.[8]

So it's logical that while the defeat of gluttony begins with the body, it is built on the Holy Spirit.

RESTRAINT IS BUILT ON THE HOLY SPIRIT

We build on the Holy Spirit by *avoiding debauchery.* In the 5th chapter of Ephesians, we discover that there was a problem of drunkenness in Ephesus. But Paul was not concerned with writing a treatise on alcoholism and the use of alcohol. Rather, his concern was to deal with the results of such behavior. So he wrote, **"Do not get drunk on wine, which leads to debauchery"** (5:18). Debauchery may be an unfamiliar word, but it is a good one. It means loose living – undisciplined, unrestrained, impulsive, wild living. Debauchery is doing whatever feels good and doing it in response to any external stimuli. The same word that is used for 'debauchery' is also used to describe the Prodigal Son, who took his inheritance and participated in 'loose living' – living that was undisciplined, unrestrained, impulsive, and wild. He did what he felt like doing. He took the money and spent it, with no principles in life whatsoever (Luke 15: 11-32). It's the same lifestyle that Paul wrote about in Romans 1:18-32 when he said that people give up the glory of God as they respond to whatever excites or interests them. How many times have you heard the maxim, "If it feels good, do it?" It's an appeal to debauchery.

We avoid debauchery – we restrain ourselves – by *yielding control to the Holy Spirit*. **"Do not get drunk on wine, which leads to debauchery. Instead, be filled with the Spirit"** (Ephesians 5:18). The great preacher Martin Lloyd Jones was a medical doctor before he felt the call to go into the ministry. So as a preacher he was able to draw parallels from his medical insights. In terms of alcohol and drunkenness he pointed out the problem: alcohol is really not a stimulant. Drunkenness makes it appear like someone is stimulated, but in reality alcohol is a depressant. It depresses the highest centers in the brain, those that control everything that give us self-control, wisdom, understanding, discrimination, judgment, and balance – the powers by which we assess everything. In other words, it spoils everything that makes us behave at our very best and highest. Lloyd Jones then points out that the Holy Spirit has a different impact. He stimulates those very powers.[9] So Paul is dramatically stating that anytime we do not allow the Holy Spirit to have full control of our lives, we deaden the very senses that make us alive to Him.

Perhaps you're thinking "I'm already filled with the Spirit." You may well be – praise the Lord! But the tense of **"be filled with the Spirit"** in Ephesians 5:18 is, "to be continually filled" with the Holy Spirit. Be filled again and again and again. Make yourself available to the Spirit. I appreciate the advice of Rick Ezell who wrote that a *good way to stay available to the Holy Spirit is to live by the four F's*, which he lists as Feed, feast, fast, and focus.[10]

- FEED regularly on the Word of God. The older I get the more I regret not having spent more time in the Word. It's a tough discipline, but it is the **"...power of God unto salvation..."** Without it, I lack His power. Without it, so will you, for the Holy Spirit flows out of God's Word into hearts.
- FEAST together with – be together to celebrate with – other Christians. There is no other environment like Christ's family. If my wife and I had not been an active part of

Christ's family I shudder to think of where we, and our boys, would be now. The influence, company, and encouragement of other Christians are essential, for the Holy Spirit flows through others into our hearts.
- FAST frequently to keep your body trim and fit and your mind keen and sharp. There's a reason Jesus repeatedly went apart from the crowds and fasted and prayed – He knew that the Holy Spirit has greater access in us when we discipline ourselves.
- FOCUS on Kingdom work. Make Christ's purpose your purpose. Speak of, witness to, and represent Jesus wherever you are, whatever your circumstance. Let the Holy Spirit flow through you.

Live according to these four F's and the Holy Spirit will keep on filling you with His power.

So avoid debauchery, yield control, live by the four F's, and *believe in the power of God.* Do you believe you have the power to overcome gluttony? Paul wrote, **"For God did not give us a spirit of timidity, but a spirit of power, of love and of self-discipline"** (2 Timothy 1:7). **"Yet he (Abraham) did not waver through unbelief regarding the promise of God, but was strengthened in his faith and gave glory to God, being fully persuaded that God had power to do what he had promised"** (Romans 4:20). And always remember Paul's prayer for you: **"I pray also that...you may know...his incomparably great**

power...That power is like the working of his mighty strength, which he exerted in Christ when he raised him from the dead and seated him at his right hand in the heavenly realms..." (Ephesians 1:18-20). Believe that. For unless you believe, it will be difficult to maintain the necessary disciplines of the 4 F's. So believe that God will enter into your heart and do what He has promised to do – **"...give (you)...a spirit of power, of love and of self-discipline."** You can restrain yourself.

In fact, you can develop not just one, but 7 habits that will make you highly healthy. Just approach Jesus and allow the Spirit of God to fill you. For Jesus said, **"If you then, though you are evil, know how to give good gifts to your children, how much more will your Father in heaven give the Holy Spirit to those who ask him!"** (Luke 11:13). I invite you to ask Him right now.

I invite you to pray: Gracious Heavenly Father – I'm tired of losing the battle to sin – of doing the very things I know I shouldn't do and not doing the things I know I should do. I want to be highly healthy so I can witness to and represent You. I believe that You are willing and have the power to do what You have promised. And You have promised to give the Holy Spirit to those who ask You. So I'm asking You right now to fill me with your Holy Spirit; grant me the power to build my life on the seven habits that will keep me healthy. Come, Holy Spirit – I welcome You!

> "Breathe on me, Breath of God,
> Fill me with life anew,
> That I may love what Thou dost love
> And do what Thou wouldst do.
>
> Breath on me, Breath of God,
> Until my heart is pure,
> Until with Thee I will one will –
> To do and to endure.
>
> Breathe on me, Breath of God,
> Till I am wholly Thine,
> Till all this earthly part of me
> Glows with Thy fire divine.
>
> Breathe on me, Breath of God,
> So shall I never die,
> But live with Thee the perfect life
> Of Thine eternity.[11]

Amen.

ENDNOTES

CHAPTER 1 – DO GOOD WORKS

1. J. Oswald Sanders, Spiritual Leadership, (Chicago: Moody Press, 1967), p. 143
2. C. S. Lewis, Mere Christianity, (New York: Macmillan, 1943), p. 94
3. "Our Daily Bread", August 2, 1992
4. Cardinal John Henry Newman, Meditations on Christian Doctrine, I. Hope in God - Creator, March 7, 1848
5. The station referred to is WCSG in Grand Rapids, Michigan (91.3 FM); see www.wcsg.org

CHAPTER 2 – PRACTICE CONTENTMENT

1. Thomas Watson, Gleanings from Thomas Watson, (Morgan, PA: Soli Deo Gloria Publications, 1995)
2. Billy Graham, as quoted in Nelson's Complete Book of Stories, Illustrations, & Quotes, p. 270
3. I have been unable to identify the poet
4. Philip Yancey, Reaching for the Invisible God (Zondervan Publishing House, Grand Rapids, Michigan, 2000), p. 58
5. Dr. Timothy Brown, *"I Can Do All Things Through Christ"*, sermon published by Preaching Today, #239

6. "Day by Day", Lina Sandell Berg, Translated by Andrew L. Skoog

CHAPTER 3 – APPLY THE GOLDEN RULE

1. Frederick Buechner, <u>Wishful Thinking</u> (Harper & Row, 1973), p. 2
2. "Rock of Ages, Cleft for Me", Augustus M. Toplady
3. Max Lucado, <u>In the Grip of Grace</u>, (Word Publishing - Dallas) 1996, p. 155
4. C. S. Lewis, <u>Mere Christianity</u>, (New York: Macmillan, 1958), p. 89
5. Rosalind Goforth, <u>Climbing: Memories of a Missionary's Wife</u> (Wheaton, IL: Sword Book Club, 1940) p. 99-102 – As quoted in <u>Nelson's Complete Book of Stories, Illustrations, & Quotes</u>, p.312
6. <u>In the Grip of Grace</u>, p. 155
7. Michael J. Wilkins, <u>The New Application Commentary 5.1</u>, (Zondervan). p. 637
8. "Come, Thou Fount", Robert Robinson (words adapted)

CHAPTER 4 – FEED YOUR HUNGER

1. A word of caution is in order. I am aware that these same characteristics could be symptoms of clinical depression. In this chapter I in no way intend to imply that clinical depression is nothing more than sloth, thereby belittling it. I affirm that clinical depression is very real and that it needs special professional treatment. However, I cannot avoid listing the characteristics of sloth even though they are very similar. If you find yourself resonating consistently with some of these characteristics, and have been for some time, I urge you to seek such professional help.
2. As quoted on www.deadlysins.com/sins/sloth.html
3. Peter Kreeft, <u>Back to Virtue</u>, (Ignatius Press, San Francisco, 1986), p. 155-156
4. Kreeft, p. 157

5. William Willimon, Sinning Like a Christian, (Abingdon Press, Nashville, 2005), p. 88
6. *Context*, March 1, 1989
7. George Meuller, Pilgrim Ministries website, www.pilgrim-promo.com/ministries
8. Mrs. Charles Cowman, Streams In The Desert, (Zondervan Publishing House, Grand Rapids, Michigan), p. 227

CHAPTER 5 – AIM FOR SIMPLICITY

1. From the 2004 movie *Super Size Me*, as reported on www.MovieMinistry.com
2. Nelson's Complete Book of Stories, Illustrations, & Quotes, p. 63
2. "Stewardship Quotes", from www.generousgiving.org
3. Ibid
4. From an old edition of the *Gospel Herald* – date unknown
5. "Stewardship Quotes"
6. Rev. Richard Tigchon, Rockford Reformed Church, Rockford, Michigan
7. Epicurus, as quoted by Dr. Robin R. Meyers, The Virtue in the Vice, (Health Communications, Inc., Deerfield Beach, Florida), p. 154
8. As quoted by William Barclay, The Daily Study Bible – Gospel of Matthew, (The Saint Andrew Press, Edinburgh, 1959), p. 260
9. Rick Ezell, The 7 Sins of Highly Defective People, (Kregel Publications, Grand Rapids, Michigan), p. 102
10. Anna Olander, "If I Gained the World" (A composite translation as it appears in Praise! Our Songs and Hymns, Singspiration Music, Division of the Zondervan Corporation

CHAPTER 6 – GUARD YOUR MIND

1. Greg Asimakoupoulos, Naperville, Illinois, *Leadership*, Vol. 17, no. 1
2. www.PreachingToday.com

7 Habits of Highly Healthy People

3. Dr. William Backus, <u>What Your Counselor Never Told You</u>, (Bethany House, Minneapolis, Minnesota, 2000), p. 166
4. www.PreachingToday.com
5. <u>A. C. Green: Standing Tall,</u> (Christian Reader – Jan/Feb 2002), pp 18-25
6. J. Oswald Sanders, <u>A Spiritual Clinic</u> (Chicago: Moody Press, 1961), p. 20
7. Leslie Flynn, as quoted in <u>Nelson's Complete Book of Stories, Illustrations, & Quotes</u>, p. 554
8. John Piper, <u>A Passion for Purity versus Passive Prayers</u>, www.desiringGod.org (11-10-99), quoted from www.PreachingToday.com
9. "When I Survey the Wondrous Cross", Isaac Watts

CHAPTER 7 – RESTRAIN YOURSELF

1. C. S. Lewis, <u>The Lion, the Witch and the Wardrobe</u>, as quoted in www.PreachingToday.com
2. John Beukema, as reported in www.PreachingToday.com
3. Rick Ezell, <u>The 7 Sins of Highly Defective People</u>, (Kregel Publications, Grand Rapids, Michigan, 2003), pp. 128-129
4. Fulton J. Sheen, <u>The Seven Capital Sins</u>, (Alba House), p. 51
5. As quoted in Dr. William Backus, <u>What Your Counselor Never Told You</u>, (Bethany House, Minneapolis, Minnesota, 2000), p. 208
6. Dr. Robin R. Meyers, <u>The Virtue in the Vice</u>, (Health Communications, Inc., Deerfield Beach, Florida), p.117
7. Ibid, p.122
8. <u>Discipleship Journal</u>, November / December, 1992 – as referenced in www.sermoncentral.com
9. Dr. Martyn Lloyd-Jones, <u>Life in the Spirit in Marriage, Home & Work, An exposition of Ephesians 5:18-6:9</u>, (Baker Book House, Grand Rapids, Michigan, July 1987), pp/ 11-25
10. <u>The 7 Sins of Highly Defective People</u>, pp. 132-134
11. "Breath on Me, Breath of God", Edwin Hatch

CPSIA information can be obtained
at www.ICGtesting.com
Printed in the USA
FFOW04n1633140317
33437FF